ATLANTA
classic
DESSERTS

ATLANTA *classic* DESSERTS

Recipes from
Favorite Restaurants

KRISTA REESE

Foreword by Janice Shay

Photography by Deborah Whitlaw Llewellyn

PELICAN PUBLISHING COMPANY
Gretna 2009

Editing by Anne Michele Williams, Betsey Brairton, Andrea Chesman, and Sara LeVere
Production by Angela Rojas

ISBN-13: 978-1-58980-621-4

Layout based on a design by Kit Wohl

Printed in China

Published by Pelican Publishing Company, Inc.
1000 Burmaster, Gretna, Louisiana 70053

To Billy: A living recipe
for sweetie pie.

CONTENTS

Chapter 4   PUDDINGS & CUSTARDS

Chapter 5   ICE CREAM, ICES & GELATO

FOREWORD

Southern cuisine may be loosely defined as the culinary tradition south of the Mason-Dixon line, but it is as varied as it is delicious, deriving its unique flavors from the influence of the Native American, British, Irish, Spanish, French, and African cultures. There are dishes synonymous with the South as a whole—think collard greens and cobblers—as well as separate culinary traditions unto themselves, such as Soul Food, Cajun, Creole, Low Country, and Appalachian Mountain cuisines.

The European settlers imported many of their baking items, like wheat flour, but sugar and molasses were locally available and the tradition of combining cornbread and molasses soon began. Local fruits also determined the development of early Southern cuisine as settlers and natives alike discovered the abundance of berries, including muscadines, blackberries, raspberries, and cherries, which would later become the basis of many classic Southern desserts.

Plantations were successful in farming cotton by the 18th century, sugar by the mid-18th century, and rice shortly thereafter. Along with the easy access to sugar and rice, which would become integral to Southern food, the early 19th century saw a revolution in kitchen technology that allowed for more precise and intricate dishes.

Because travel was difficult, rural Southerners held large barbecues and oyster roasts to bring together neighbors from the extended plantations and homesteads for visits that would last days, if not weeks. The menus included everything from jellied veal and ham pie and goose in aspic, to a plethora of desserts, including peach ice, cherry bounce, and trifle with syllabub.

After the Civil War, Southern cooks made the best of the cheapest ingredients available. The result was beloved dishes like gumbos, fried vegetables, and bread puddings, using stale breads to create a sweet dessert that still shows up on many menus.

Over the last 20 years, New Southern cuisine has emerged on the culinary scene and Atlanta has become its epicenter. Atlanta's extraordinary concentration of restaurants, combined with the fact that its metro area has grown by more than 40 percent in 10 years, has made it a perfect environment for the new and the old to come together and invent cutting-edge dishes that hold true to our Southern roots—much as the natives and settlers of the area did hundreds of years ago.

The concept of Southern cuisine remained largely a bypassed genre in the world of gourmet cooking until Nathalie Dupree's 1986 cookbook *New Southern Cooking*. Dupree, a resident of Atlanta, introduced classic Southern comfort foods with new high-end, cultural, and healthy twists, onto the world stage. Now, New Southern cuisine is part of our culinary lexicon.

The evolution of Southern cuisine continues as beloved favorites are renovated, but never reinvented, in the veritable laboratories of Atlanta's finest restaurants. While Georgia's pecan pies may no longer be cooked on a hearth and cooled in a window, Wysteria's Pecan Pie with Ginger Whipped Cream is served to enthusiastic diners; Mary Mac's Tea Room features the famed and ever-fabulous Georgia peanut in its Peanut Butter Pie. These are, of course, just two examples of the delicious goodies to be found in this book. Enjoy!

—*Janice Shay*

INTRODUCTION

Is there such a thing as an Atlanta classic… anything? Sometimes it seems the speed and fervor with which we tear down the old and replace it with something new might make even our city's symbol, the phoenix, fear he may be next.

What Sherman started we've continued—sometimes to the point of losing small bits of our collective heart and soul. Sure, there's plenty to celebrate—the Braves, the revered universities, the Martin Luther King Center, the Jimmy Carter Center, CNN, Coca-Cola, our bustling airport, and leafy, walkable neighborhoods. But, aside from change itself, one of Atlanta's most enduring cultural legacies is its food.

For almost 20 years, I've had the privilege of sampling and observing Atlanta's restaurants, and being paid to write about them. With a cloak of invisibility Harry Potter couldn't duplicate (I'm a white woman in my 50s), I've had a discreet view of this difficult, heart-breaking and occasionally very lucrative business. The food scene is a fascinating microcosm of what Atlanta has become: sophisticated, wildly diverse, malleable enough to bear the marks of other cultures, but with an identity strong enough to withstand a global onslaught. I could never have dreamed how far and how fast Atlanta's dining scene would progress, so that it now rivals that of much larger American cities like Chicago or Los Angeles. Today our mosaic of immigrant restaurants includes Eritrean, Moroccan, Peruvian and Slovakian.

Despite my Southern family and schooling, there are a few things I missed when I moved here from New York in 1988: A good bagel. Chow fun. Jewel-box specialty shops like Dean & Deluca and Balducci's. And, especially, exotic ethnic restaurants such as the Burmese place next door to me in SoHo, or the Cuban-Chinese joints in the West Village.

While in New York, of course, I longed for tastes of home. And when I did, the bites I craved most were the sweets. Each city or region has its specialties, and it seems Atlanta's most popular are the fodder of most recipe books—cakes, pies, cookies and pud-

dings—but with a twist. Leave the beautifully layered trifles and gorgeous soufflés to Charleston and New Orleans, and from Atlanta make way for the specialty cake—created by professionals, layered with berries, frosted in butter cream, pooled in chocolate sauce. Most of us stuck-in-traffic folks have a jones for those banana puddings and Hummingbird cakes of our youths, but Atlanta is the City Too Busy to Bake. Perhaps syllabubs, pandowdies and ambrosias once ruled here, but the cake has outlasted them all, surviving in ever-more glorious forms. Even the old-fashioned recipes from Mary Mac's and the Colonnade have a once-in-a-blue-moon quality of fussy richness—and one of my great regrets was learning that the Varsity Drive-In never, ever gives out its fried pie recipe.

Atlanta's first Grande Dame of cookery was Mrs. Henrietta Dull, a widow who turned to cooking to raise her children, and in 1928, compiled one of the first basic Southern cookbooks, *Southern Cooking*. Though it's often short on details (one cake's directions read, simply "Mix as any cake. Bake 1 1/2 hours in tube pan."), Mrs. Dull's cookbook arrived just in time to rescue a generation of cooks who had no servants, no skills, and no guidance. The cookbook is still in print, and the largest portion of its dessert chapter is taken up with pies and cakes.

Even today in Atlanta, when we sample another culture's cuisine, we use the familiar as a touchstone. We want to try Taqueria Los Hermanos' Tres Leches Cake, layered with fresh fruit. We indulge in the Ritz-Carlton Dining Room's elevation of our native muscadines to a world-class delicacy. And, we want our own specialties revised into something familiar, but entirely novel, like Richard Blais' Pecan Cake with Sweet Tea Ice Cream.

It makes perfect seense that Atlantans would fall in love w ith these re-invented sweets and baked goods. After all, we've become expert at using fire to transform the old into something entirely new.

—*Krista Reese*

On the move: Atlanta's landmark Richard Meier-designed High Museum of Art expanded in 2005, with three new buildings by architect Renzo Piano, and a piazza for Roy Lichtenstein's cozy little House III.

CANDY, COOKIES & DOUGHNUTS

Atlanta is all about movement, so it seems appropriate that portable treats like cookies and candies are quintessential Atlanta sweets. Stick 'em in your mouth, and go! But these roaming tidbits have been domesticated, evolving into sophisticated sit-down courses, best approached with a fork, spoon, and large napkin. Trickled with sauces, topped with exotic ice creams, here they are very serious dishes. But like the best people, each of these miniature delicacies has the soul of a little kid.

THE GLENWOOD ATLANTA
FRIED OREOS WITH BOURBON ICE CREAM

Inspired by the funnel cakes at the state fair, this recipe is made with Double-Stuf Oreos. The truly adventurous can use their favorite candy bar or a Twinkie instead.

SERVES 6

BOURBON ICE CREAM
2 cups heavy cream
2 cups milk
1 cup sugar
1/4 to 1/2 cup bourbon
1 vanilla bean, split lengthwise and scraped
12 large egg yolks

FRIED OREOS
2 cups all-purpose flour
1/2 teaspoon baking powder

1/2 teaspoon salt
2 tablespoons confectioners' sugar
5 ice cubes
About 2 cups seltzer
1 egg yolk
1 (18-ounce) package Double-Stuf Oreo cookies
Vegetable shortening for deep-frying

Confectioners' sugar, to garnish
Fresh mint leaves, to garnish
Raspberries, to garnish

Our town has two trademarks: leafy neighborhoods, and the flight of the phoenix (symbolizing rebirth). Well, that bird sure landed here; the incredible resurgence of the Glenwood's charming nabe, East Atlanta Village, is due almost entirely to the young, creative talents who moved here to paint, to sing… and to cook. Over the last decade clever, fun-loving restaurants run by pioneering young restaurateurs fueled the revival of this once-desolate 1920s crossroads, and the Glenwood is a fine example of the next generation. Cool, hip and innovative, it demonstrates that even this forever-young neighborhood can show surprising maturity. The menu features both pimento cheese and a bento box. With a large bar and casual atmosphere, the Glenwood is designed to accommodate the fine art of hanging out.

To prepare the ice cream, combine the cream, milk, and 1/2 cup of the granulated sugar in a saucepan. Add bourbon to taste (but do not exceed 1/2 cup or the mixture will not freeze). Add the vanilla bean. Bring to a boil.

In a medium bowl, beat together the egg yolks and remaining 1/2 cup granulated sugar. Very slowly add about half the cream mixture, whisking constantly. Whisk the yolk mixture into the saucepan and cook over medium heat until the custard coats the back of a spoon.

Strain through a fine sieve and chill, preferably overnight. Freeze in an ice-cream maker according to the manufacturer's instructions.

To prepare the batter for the fried Oreos, mix together the flour, baking powder, salt, and confectioners' sugar in a medium bowl. Put the 5 ice cubes in a glass measuring cup and add enough seltzer to make 2 cups. Add to the flour mixture along with the egg yolk. Mix until there are no large lumps and the ice cubes have melted. Set aside.

Fill a tall saucepan or deep-fryer with up to 2 inches of vegetable shortening and heat to 350° F. Dip the Oreos in the batter and fry a few at a time until crispy, 45 to 60 seconds. Carefully remove with a slotted spoon and drain on paper towels. Continue until all the Oreos have been batter-dipped and fried.

To serve, place three Oreos on each plate with a scoop of ice cream in the center. Sprinkle with confectioners' sugar and garnish with mint and fresh raspberries.

SHAUN'S RESTAURANT
RICOTTA ZEPPOLES, SAN GENNARO STYLE

This dish is Shaun's tribute to Little Italy's Feast of San Gennaro, and the little fried-dough dirigible called a zeppole.

SERVES 6

ZEPPOLES
2 cups all-purpose flour
2 cups whole milk ricotta cheese
1 1/2 tablespoons baking powder
1 tablespoon granulated sugar
1/2 teaspoon salt
4 large eggs
Vegetable oil, for deep-frying
Confectioners' sugar, for dusting

CHOCOLATE SAUCE
8 ounces dark chocolate, coarsely chopped
1 cup heavy cream
1/2 cup corn syrup

CARAMEL SAUCE
2 cups granulated sugar
1/3 cup unsalted butter
3 cups heavy cream

To prepare the zeppole batter, mix together the flour, ricotta, baking powder, granulated sugar, and eggs until smooth.

To prepare the chocolate sauce, put the chocolate in a heatproof bowl. Heat the cream and corn syrup in saucepan over medium high heat until boiling. Pour over the chocolate and whisk until smooth. Keep warm to serve.

To prepare the caramel sauce, put the granulated sugar in a heavy-bottom saucepan over high heat. Stirring constantly and carefully, cook until the sugar is melted and turns a dark amber color. Add the butter to sugar and stir until melted. Add the cream, a little at a time, and whisk until smooth. Once all the cream is added, allow the mixture to return to a boil. Lower the heat and reduce the caramel sauce to a desired consistency.

Keep warm.

Heat the vegetable oil in a tall saucepan or deep-fryer to 350° F. Spoon mounds of the dough, 1/4 to 1/2 inch in diameter, directly into hot oil, being careful to avoid splashing. Carefully rotate the zeppoles in the oil to cook evenly on all sides. Fry until golden brown and remove from the oil with slotted spoon. Drain immediately on paper towels. Dust with generous amounts of confectioners' sugar.

Serve hot, with the chocolate and caramel sauces drizzled over the zeppoles.

Atlantans have watched Shaun Doty's cooking career mature before their eyes. The young chef went from wunderkind and creative spark at a string of restaurants (Mumbo Jumbo, MidCity Cuisine, Table 1280), to restaurateur at his own thriving hotspot in Inman Park. With a color scheme of washed whites and calming greens, a rock-on soundtrack, and a seasonal, regional American menu as cosmopolitan as our town, Shaun's attracts Atlanta's well-heeled Bohemian crowd, as well as critical raves from the likes of Esquire, Bon Appetit, Food & Wine, Atlanta Journal-Constitution, *and* Atlanta *magazine. Dishes include tips of the toque to Georgia, as well as Maryland, New York, Charleston… and that great American region, Chinatown.*

ARIA
S'MORES

SERVES 12

GRAHAM CRACKERS
3/4 cup whole-wheat flour
2 1/2 cups all-purpose flour
1 1/4 cups confectioners' sugar
1/2 teaspoon ground cinnamon
1/2 teaspoon ground cardamom
1/2 teaspoon ground ginger
2 sticks unsalted butter, chilled and diced into
    1/2-inch pieces
3 large egg yolks
1/8 teaspoon salt
3/4 teaspoon vanilla extract
1 teaspoon molasses

CHOCOLATE LAYER
8 ounces good-quality bittersweet or
    dark chocolate
4 Heath Bars, finely chopped

MARSHMALLOWS
1 cup cold water
8 1/2 teaspoons unflavored gelatin powder
2 cups granulated sugar
1/2 cup light corn syrup
1/4 teaspoon salt
2 egg whites
1 teaspoon vanilla extract
Confectioners' sugar, to dust

Romantic, sophisticated, understated … Aria seems to fly under the radar, quietly and consistently delivering luscious, slow-cooked fare with unpretentious service and a healthy sense of humor. For the last eight years, chef / owner Gary Klaskala and pastry chef Kathryn King (both former art students) have drawn an interesting mix of Atlanta's diverse achievers, who know they can dine in privacy in the low-key glow of the off-white dining room. Having been named one of the country's best by Esquire and among Atlanta's top five by Gayot, Aria specializes in patiently pulling out the inner deliciousness of a root vegetable or braised meat, and making it all look easy. King has earned special praise for her chocolate desserts. It's impossible to describe the dining experience here without using the word "sexy."

To prepare the graham crackers, combine the whole-wheat flour, all-purpose flour, confectioners' sugar, cinnamon, cardamom, and ginger in a large mixing bowl and mix well with an electric mixer. Add the butter all at once, and mix on low speed until the mixture looks sandy.

In a small bowl, mix together the egg yolks, salt, vanilla, and molasses. Add to the dry mixture and mix until just incorporated. Turn the dough out onto a sheet of plastic wrap, press into a 1-inch-thick rectangle, and chill for at least 1 hour.

Cover a work surface with parchment paper or waxed paper. Roll out the dough into a rectangular shape about 1/8 inch thick. Transfer the paper to a sheet pan. Chill for 1 hour.

Using a knife or pizza cutter, cut the dough into 24 even-size squares. Place the squares onto two baking sheets lined with parchment paper and put in the freezer until it is firm.

Preheat the oven to 350° F.

Bake the crackers, right from the freezer, for 10 minutes or until lightly browned. Cool completely on wire racks. Store in an airtight container if not using immediately.

To prepare the chocolate layer, melt the chocolate in a heatproof bowl set in a pan of barely simmering water. Add the Heath bars and stir. Spread as thinly as possible onto parchment paper or waxed paper. Cover with another sheet of parchment or waxed paper. Chill until set.

Peel off the paper from both sides of the chocolate. Let the chocolate warm slightly, then cut into the same size squares as the graham crackers. Refrigerate until you are ready to assemble the dessert.

To prepare the marshmallows, pour 1 cup of the the cold water into the bowl of an electric mixer and sprinkle the gelatin over the water. Set aside for 5 minutes to soften.

Oil an 11-inch by 17-inch baking pan and dust with confectioners' sugar.

Combine the remaining 1 cup water, sugar, corn syrup, and salt in a heavy nonreactive saucepan and bring to a boil. Continue to boil until the mixture reaches 240° F on a candy thermometer. Im-

mediately pour the hot syrup over the gelatin mixture and beat until tripled in volume.

In a separate bowl, beat the egg whites and vanilla until stiff peaks form. Fold into the sugar mixture. Pour into the prepared pan. Dust the top with more confectioners' sugar. Refrigerate for 2 hours, or until set. Cut to the same size as the graham crackers. Cover with plastic wrap until you are ready to use it.

To assemble the dessert, place 12 crackers on a baking sheet. Place one cut piece of chocolate on each cracker. Top the chocolate with a cut piece of marshmallow.

Brown with a kitchen blowtorch or under a hot broiler. Top with the second cracker. Enjoy soon after melting, but watch out for the heat.

BISTRO VG
Molten Chocolate Fritters

SERVES 10 TO 12

RASPBERRY PUREE
2 pints raspberries
Finely grated zest and juice of 1 orange
3/4 cup granulated sugar
1 vanilla bean, split and scraped
1/2 cup raspberry liqueur

FRITTERS
3/4 cup granulated sugar
4 large eggs
14 tablespoons butter, melted
2 cups all-purpose flour
1 cup unsweetened cocoa powder
1 tablespoon baking powder

FRITTER SUGAR
2 1/3 cups confectioners' sugar
1/3 cup unsweetened cocoa powder

Oil, for deep-frying
Vanilla ice cream, to serve
Fresh raspberries, to serve

To prepare the raspberry puree, combine the raspberries, orange zest and juice, 3/4 cup granulated sugar, the seeds from the vanilla bean, and raspberry liqueur in a saucepan. Cook over medium heat until soupy. Strain the mixture through a fine-mesh sieve. Measure out 1 cup. Reserve the remainder.

To prepare the fritters, whisk together the granulated sugar and eggs. Add the melted butter and whisk just to combine. Mix in the 1 cup raspberry puree. Sift the flour, cocoa, and baking powder over the egg mixture. Fold in until just incorporated. Cover and refrigerate for 1 hour.

To prepare the fritter sugar, sift together the confectioners' sugar and cocoa.

Heat the oil in a tall saucepan or deep-fryer until it reaches 300° F on a deep-frying thermometer. Form the dough into balls the size of golf balls and fry a few at a time for 2 to 3 minutes, or until they float to the surface. Immediately dredge in the fritter sugar. Continue until all the dough is used.

Garnish each serving with the reserved raspberry puree, ice cream, and fresh raspberries.

The suburbs' first great restaurant continues its evolution. Christopher and Michele Sedgwick opened their Roswell boite in 1991 as Van Gogh's (and continued the arty theme with sibling efforts Theo's Bakery and Vinny's on Windward). Back then, suburbanites were content to raise their kids in sweeping green spaces outside the Perimeter, driving into town when they wanted fine wine and memorable food. Van Gogh's changed all that with a gorgeous interior, award-winning wine list, and a menu as inventive and sophisticated as anything on Peachtree Street. Renamed and redesigned in 2007 as Bistro VG, the restaurant's interior is now even more sensuous, with a white-on-white scheme of textures that includes Venetian plaster, a patent leather-walled nook, and European linens. The menu is still classic French bistro and, appropriately enough for its namesake, Bistro VG's studious re-inventions of desserts like clafoutis and tarte tatin have been described as "painterly."

Chef Camerino's El Ray Milk Chocolate Caramel with Hawaiian Black Lava Salt

Chef Camerino chose El Ray milk chocolate for its buttery richness. El Ray is a single-origin chocolate company located in Venezuela. Their practices are fair trade and environmentally conscious.

YIELDS 40 PIECES

CARAMEL
8 ounces El Ray milk chocolate, coarsely chopped
1/4 ounce cocoa butter
3 tablespoons water
1/3 cup granulated sugar
2/3 cup heavy cream
1 1/2 teaspoons corn syrup
1 1/2 tablespoons unsalted butter, at room temperature
1/4 teaspoon Hawaiian black lava salt

FINISH
Black cocoa or Cacoa Barry Extra Brut Cocoa
Hawaiian black lava salt

"By young people, for young people and friendly to the rest of us." This quirky little space with the upstairs dining room is the ambitious enterprise of some creative upstarts, undaunted by the prospect of overcoming such obstacles as heights, missing vowels or conventional attitudes. The globally conscious, very affordable menu touches down in Thailand, Lebanon, Italy and the good old U.S. of A., never sacrificing taste for novelty. Even the most exotic dishes (like pan-roasted, ginger-crusted tofu with pomegranate miso dressing) have the down-home deliciousness of another menu standby: mac 'n' cheese. If you're short of time or breath, reserve a downstairs table, or drop by for a drink at the lower-level bar. Better yet, swing by for a late-night (or early morning) dessert. The all-chocolate desserts by pastry chef Taria Camerino include exquisite truffles whose delicate appearance belie their tasty wallop.

Line an 8-inch square baking dish with plastic wrap.

Combine the chocolate and cocoa butter in a stainless bowl; set aside.

Combine the water and sugar in a heavy-bottomed saucepan and cook over medium heat until the sugar melts and turns a dark amber color. Meanwhile, combine the cream and corn syrup in a saucepan and bring to a light simmer. When the sugar is a dark amber, very slowly pour the cream mixture into the sugar, mixing well as you go. Pour the mixture over the chocolate and cocoa butter and mix until thoroughly blended. The consistency should be like homemade mayonnaise. Cool to lukewarm (95° F on an instant-read thermometer). Stir in the butter. Pour into the prepared cake pan, spread evenly, and knock the pan against the counter to release air bubbles. Freeze for 2 hours, until set.

Sift 1/2 cup cocoa into deep dish or pan, pour salt into small bowl for easy access.

Once the chocolate ganache is firm, remove from freezer. Unmold by pulling up on the plastic wrap, remove the plastic, and place on a cutting board. Cut into 40 pieces (5 rows by 8 rows). Gently roll the ganache rectangles into the cocoa powder, pressing lightly on bottoms and sides to ensure coating. Remove and place on a papered surface, sprinkle 3 to 4 grains of the salt on top, and press the salt into top. Keep chilled at 45° to 60° F.

NOTE: If desired, you can dip chocolates in tempered milk chocolate before rolling in cocoa.

Eating it too: Wedding-cake fancy, the Fox Theater was one of the first historic buildings Atlantans united to save from the wrecking ball. Today the former 1930s Moorish movie palace is one of the city's most popular destinations.

CAKES

Other Southern cities (see Charleston, Savannah, New Orleans) seem to favor elegant trifles and custards. But perhaps Atlanta's favorite dessert is cake—rare is the restaurant without two or three on the dessert list, from strictly Southern concoctions like angel food cake to new takes on old favorites, like the Sweet Tea Ice Cream on Richard Blais' Sour Cream Pecan Cake.

LEMON POPPYSEED CAKE

SERVES 8

1 1/4 cups sugar
Zest of 2 lemons
2 teaspoons fresh lemon juice
4 large eggs
1 1/2 teaspoons vanilla extract
1 cup unsalted butter, melted
1 1/2 cups all-purpose flour
1 teaspoon baking powder
1/2 teaspoon salt
2 tablespoons poppy seeds

GLAZE
1/2 cup sugar
1/4 cup fresh lemon juice

LEMON MOUSSE
4 large eggs, separated
3/4 cup sugar
1/2 cup fresh lemon juice
1 tablespoon finely grated lemon zest
1 1/2 teaspoons unflavored gelatin powder
2 tablespoons water
1/2 cup heavy cream

Preheat the oven to 325° F. Butter and flour a 9-inch by 5-inch loaf pan.

To prepare the cake, combine the sugar and lemon zest in a food processor and pulse until the zest is finely chopped. Add the lemon juice, eggs, and vanilla and pulse until combined, about 5 seconds. With the motor running, slowly pour in the melted butter; this should take about 20 seconds. Transfer the mixture to a large stainless bowl. Combine the flour, baking powder, and salt and sift over the egg mixture. Add the poppy seeds and whisk until well combined. Pour into the prepared pan.

Bake for 15 minutes. Lower the oven temperature to 300° F and continue baking for about 45 minutes, until a skewer inserted in the center comes out clean. Remove from the oven and let cool for 10 minutes.

To prepare the glaze, combine the sugar and lemon juice in a nonreactive saucepan and simmer until the sugar is dissolved. Turn the cake out onto a rack and dot with holes. Brush the sugar and lemon mixture over the cake. Let cool completely.

To prepare the lemon mousse, combine the egg yolks and 1/2 cup of the sugar in an electric mixer fitted with a whip attachment and beat until pale and a ribbon is formed. Stir in the lemon juice and transfer to a heatproof bowl. Place the bowl in a pan of simmering water and cook, stirring constantly, until the mixture reaches 160° F on an instant-read thermometer. Remove from the heat and strain. Stir in the lemon zest. Let cool to room temperature.

Sprinkle the gelatin over the water in a small heatproof bowl. Let soften for 10 minutes. Set the bowl in a pan of barely simmering water and stir until the gelatin completely dissolves. Stir the gelatin into the yolk mixture.

Beat the egg whites in the bowl of an electric mixer on low speed until frothy. Slowly add the remaining 1/4 cup sugar and increase the speed to high, beating to soft peaks. Add one-third of the beaten whites to the yolk mixture; stir in to lighten.

Beat the cream with the electric mixer to soft peaks. Add the yolk mixture and remaining egg whites and fold together. Pour into 9-inch square baking pan. Refrigerate for at least 2 hours.

To serve, slice the poppy seed cake into eight portions. Place each slice on a serving plate and add a scoop of lemon mousse to the plate.

Chef-owner Marla Adams' charming little cafe is all about the spaces in-between: between funky Poncey-Highland and Victorian Inman Park; between strict French and relaxed Catalonian fare; between fine dining and a summer picnic. So dedicated to fresh produce is this restaurant that the small house also serves as a neighborhood pick-up for community-supported agriculture deliveries. Babette's is a feast (yes, it's named for the book and movie) of newly picked flavors, informed by Adams' traditional European techniques. This house is home to a devoted corps of regulars, who began dining at Babette's 14 years ago, in a smaller space farther down Highland Avenue. The current location is painted in sun-washed Provençal colors and has a large back deck overlooking Freedom Parkway. You've got to love a restaurant owner so generous with her customers that she will gladly email them her recipes, but warns on her website, "Any parent allowing their child to become a nuisance will be flogged."

RESTAURANT AND TAPAS LOUNGE

Nearly as exciting as the High Museum's expansion in 2006—which allowed it to land such prestigious exhibitions as the three-year collaboration with the Louvre Museum in Paris—is the addition of this utterly cool, completely clever restaurant across from its entrance. Like the High's new wing, Table 1280 was designed by famed architect Renzo Piano (in association with the Bergmeyer Associates, who assisted with the restaurant), with a stark construction of concrete, wood, leather and white walls featuring exuberant displays of contemporary art. Like the Modern, the restaurant sidekick to New York's Museum of Modern Art, Table 1280 successfully captures the joy of the new one might experience at an exciting exhibition. It's also a fascinating habitat, with glass expanses framing a biosphere of beautiful, intriguing diners. The food is as witty and clever as the environment is exacting.

TABLE 1280
ANGEL FOOD CAKE WITH SHERBET AND LAVENDER CREAM

SERVES 12

ANGEL FOOD CAKE
12 egg whites, at room temperature
1/3 cup water
1/2 teaspoon vanilla extract
1/2 teaspoon bitter almond extract
1 1/2 teaspoons cream of tartar
1 3/4 cups sugar
1 cup all-purpose flour
1/4 teaspoon salt

LEMONGRASS SHERBET
5 lemongrass stems, chopped
8 cups whole milk
4 cups sugar
Pinch of salt

LAVENDER CREAM
2 cups heavy cream
1/2 cup sugar
1 tablespoon dried lavender
1/2 vanilla bean, split lengthwise and scraped
4 large egg yolks

RASPBERRY COULIS
1 cup raspberries
1/2 cup sugar
½ cup water
prigs of mint, to garnish

Preheat the oven to 350° F.

To prepare the cake, combine the egg whites, water, vanilla extract, almond extract, cream of tartar and half the sugar in a large bowl. Whip until medium peaks form. Sift the flour, salt, and remaining sugar on top of the whites and fold in until incorporated. Ladle the ingredients into an ungreased 12-inch Bundt pan. Take a skewer and run through the batter to ensure uniform distribution.

Bake for 30 minutes, or until a skewer inserted into the cake comes out clean. Cool it upside down on a cooling rack for at least 1 hour before unmolding.

To prepare the sherbet, combine the lemongrass, milk, sugar, and salt in a saucepan and bring to a boil. Remove from the heat and allow to steep for 1 hour. Strain through a fine-mesh sieve. Freeze in an ice-cream machine according to the manufacturer's instructions. Transfer to an airtight container and freeze.

To prepare the lavender cream, combine the cream, sugar, lavender, and seeds from the vanilla bean in a saucepan and bring to a boil. Whisk the yolks in a bowl. Gradually whisk in about half the hot cream mixture into the yolks. Return to the saucepan and cook over medium heat until the mixture thickens slightly and coats the back of a spoon. Let it cool, then chill before serving.

To make the raspberry coulis, combine the raspberries, sugar, and water in a saucepan and bring to a full boil for 5 minutes, stirring occasionally. Puree in a blender and strain.

To serve, spoon 2 tablespoons of the lavender cream into the center of each plate. Place a slice of cake on top. Toss the fresh raspberries in the raspberry coulis and place on either side of the cake. Finish with a scoop of sherbet and garnish with a sprig of mint.

TAQUERIA LOS HERMANOS
TRES LECHES CAKE

SERVES 12

1 (18.5-ounce) box white cake mix
3 large eggs
1/3 cup vegetable oil
1 1/4 cups water
2 cups heavy cream
3/4 cup condensed milk
3/4 cup evaporated milk
1/2 cup confectioners' sugar
1 teaspoon vanilla extract
1 cup pineapple chopped into 1/2-inch pieces
1 cup strawberries chopped into 1/2-inch
    pieces
1 cup halved seedless red grapes

Prepare the cake mix, adding the eggs, oil, and water and baking according to directions for sheet cake. Cool completely.

Combine 3/4 cup of the cream, the condensed milk, and evaporated milk in a spouted measuring cup or pitcher. With a knife, lightly scrape the surface of the cake to loosen the crust, which allows the milk mixture to penetrate better. Do not remove the scraped crust. Gradually pour the three-quarters of the milk mixture over the cake, using a pastry brush to distribute it evenly and letting it soak in to the cake. Pour the remaining milk mixture over the cake and allow to soak in. Set aside.

Combine the remaining 1 1/4 cups cream, confectioners' sugar, and vanilla in a mixing bowl. Beat with an electric mixer until stiff peaks form. Spread over the cake. Arrange the fruit on top of the whipped cream. Chill for at least 1 hour before serving.

This modest strip-mall storefront quickly became a neighborhood favorite in the Atlanta satellite village of Tucker by offering creative alternatives to standard-issue Tex-Mex. The five Ballesteros hermanos (brothers) have since expanded and added a second, larger location. In addition to some of the best low-cost California-style Mexican food and soft tacos in town, Taqueria los Hermanos features tamales handmade by Mama Ballesteros every Saturday. But what really makes the place stand out are Miguel Ballesteros' desserts: True, eggy flans, dribbled with Kahlua; bread pudding, made with traditional Mexican bread and cinnamon, soaked in tequila; and a tres leches cake that takes this "three-milk" (fresh, evaporated, and condensed) standard to a new high with the addition of fresh fruit.

With a reputation almost as large as his profile, Kevin Rathbun took the city by storm with his namesake restaurant, which is as boisterous and crackling with energy as his food is bold and transformative. There's nothing half-hearted or dispassionate about this place—from the dark, dramatic dining room to the Zen-like patio, to the menu's all-American flavors: lots of gutsy red meat and potatoes, but plenty of respect for fresh vegetables and gentle textures too. Cooking and creativity are Rathbun family traits; brother Kent is a chef in Dallas (the two teamed up to beat Bobby Flay on "Iron Chef America") and their mother ran restaurants in Kansas City, where their father was a jazz musician. That Midwestern eye for great beef and an appreciation for regional cuisines has translated into other Rathbun enterprises (Rathbun Steak; and Krog Bar, with small, tasty plates), and some of the city's highest restaurant honors, including nods from Travel & Leisure, Esquire and Bon Appetit, as well as from regional publications like Atlanta magazine and Georgia Trend.

RATHBUN'S
GOOEY TOFFEE CAKE, JACK DANIEL'S ICE CREAM

SERVES 10

GOOEY TOFFEE CAKE
6 ounces pitted dates
1 1/4 cups water
1 teaspoon baking soda
1 1/2 cups all-purpose flour
1 teaspoon baking powder
1/2 cup unsalted butter
3/4 cup granulated sugar
2 large eggs
1 teaspoon vanilla extract

TOFFEE SAUCE
2 1/2 cup firmly packed light brown sugar
7 tablespoons unsalted butter

1 cup half-and-half
1 tablespoon brandy
1 teaspoon vanilla extract
6 ounces Heath bar bits

TOASTED PECAN ICE CREAM
1 1/2 cups pecan pieces
3 cups milk
1 cinnamon stick
1/2 vanilla bean, split lengthwise and scraped
6 large eggs
1 cup granulated sugar
1/2 cup sour cream
1/2 teaspoon whiskey

Preheat the oven to 325° F. Spray a 9-inch by 3-inch springform pan with nonstick cooking spray.

To prepare the cake, combine the dates and water in a saucepan and bring to a boil. Turn off the heat, gradually add the baking soda (it will foam), and set aside.

Sift together the flour and baking powder.

Cream the butter and granulated sugar with an electric mixer until light and fluffy. With the mixer running, add 1 egg and mix until incorporated. Add the remaining egg and vanilla and continue to mix until smooth. Add the flour mixture in thirds, alternating with the date mixture. Beat until all is combined and smooth. Pour into the prepared baking pans.

Bake for 20 minutes, or until toothpick inserted into the center of one of the cakes comes out clean. Cool completely on wire racks.

Preheat the oven to 400° F.

To prepare the toffee sauce, combine the brown sugar, butter, half-and-half, and brandy in a saucepan and bring to a boil. Boil for 3 minutes. Add the vanilla and Heath bar bits and stir until almost smooth. Ladle equal amounts of the hot sauce over the cooled cakes.

Bake for 5 minutes, or until bubbly and golden. Remove from the oven and decrease the heat to 350° F. Let the cakes cool to room temperature.

To prepare the ice cream, spread out the pecans in a single layer on a baking sheet. Toast for 6 to 8 minutes, until lightly colored and fragrant.

Combine the milk, cinnamon stick, and vanilla in a saucepan and bring to a boil. Toss the nuts into the milk mixture. Remove from the heat and let rest for at least 10 minutes.

Prepare an ice bath by placing a small bowl into a large bowl of ice; this is to rapidly cool down

the ice-cream mixture. Add 1/2 cup of the granulated sugar to the milk mixture and bring to a boil. Meanwhile, whisk the remaining 1/2 cup granulated sugar with the egg yolks until lemony in color. Gradually add the hot milk mixture to the egg yolk mixture, whisking constantly. Return to the saucepan and cook over low heat until slightly thickened, 2 to 3 minutes, stirring with a spatula so as not to create air bubbles. Pour through the strainer into the ice bath to cool down the mixture rapidly. Freeze in an ice-cream machine according to the manufacturer's directions.

Let the toffee cake cool at room temperature for 2 hours. Release from the springform pan and slice. Heat each slice in a microwave for 20 seconds at full power to warm. Top with toasted pecan ice cream, garnish with mint, and serve.

CARVER'S COUNTRY KITCHEN
Coca-Cola Cake

SERVES 10 TO 12

COCA-COLA CAKE
2 cups sifted all-purpose flour (King Arthur
 flour is recommended)
2 cups granulated sugar
1 cup unsalted butter
1 cup Coca-Cola
2 tablespoons unsweetened cocoa powder
2 large eggs
1/2 cup buttermilk
1 teaspoon baking soda
1/2 teaspoon salt
1 teaspoon vanilla extract
1 teaspoon almond extract (optional)

COCA-COLA FROSTING
1/2 cup unsalted butter
1/3 cup Coca-Cola
3 tablespoons unsweetened cocoa powder
2 teaspoons vanilla extract
1 pound confectioners' sugar
Chopped nuts, to garnish (optional)

Preheat the oven to 350° F. Grease and flour a 9-inch by 13-inch baking dish or two 8-inch round cake pans.

To prepare the cake, sift the flour and sugar into a medium bowl.

Melt the butter in a saucepan. Stir in the Coke and cocoa powder and bring to a boil. Pour over flour mixture. Beat with an electric mixer for 2 minutes. Add the buttermilk, eggs, baking soda, salt, vanilla, and almond flavoring. Beat just until blended. The batter will be thin. Pour into prepared pan(s).

Bake for 20 minutes, or until the center of the cake springs back when lightly touched, or a toothpick comes out clean.

Cool the cake(s) on a wire rack for 10 minutes. Then invert onto the wire racks to finish cooling.

To prepare the frosting, melt the butter in a saucepan over medium heat. Pour in the Coke, cocoa powder, and vanilla. Stir until thoroughly blended. Transfer to a bowl. Beat in confectioners' sugar until the frosting is a good spreading consistency. Apply the frosting to the cake, creating one sheet cake or a layer cake. Sprinkle nuts on top, if desired.

One of the last vestiges of the blue-collar neighborhood that was Howell Station, Carver's Country Kitchen is a time capsule of … well, many things, including long marriages, country stores (you once could buy groceries here, until the food became so popular the shelves were cleared for more table space), corny sayings, knickknacks, and the days when most people worked so hard and so physically they actually needed this many calories at lunch. Sharon Carver still cooks the delectable buffet (it changes daily, but you can call to hear the recorded message of what's on tap today); her husband Robert rings up your purchase, which might include thick-sliced ham, meat loaf or brisket; baby limas, turnip greens or caramelized fried corn and, of course, a signature dessert, such as the moist Coca-Cola cake.

JCT stands for the old railroad "junction" sign chef William "Ford" Fry spied as he was trying to think of a name for this so-old-fashioned-it's-hip farmstead-style restaurant in rapidly developing west Atlanta. The materials recall a country store or 1930s kitchen: washed greys, greens, zinc, hardwoods and concrete. And the name is apt. Here's where young Bohemians' food fantasies intersect with their grandparents' in ways neither would have imagined. Never veering far from the deeply delicious selection of easily accessible Southern favorites, Fry still manages to make his menu grown-up and challenging by using local ingredients with European techniques: chicken and dumplings that have more in common with coq au vin and gnocchi; potatoes roasted in pan drippings; spinach with bacon vinaigrette. The nightly cobbler is topped with house-made peach ice cream.

JCT KITCHEN & BAR
RUM "SOPPED" COCONUT CAKE

SERVES 8 TO 10

CAKE
12 large eggs
2 cups sugar
1 teaspoon kosher or coarse salt
2 cups all-purpose flour

"SOPPING" MILK
2 1/2 cups coconut milk
2 1/2 cups sweetened condensed milk
1/3 cup dark rum
1 teaspoons almond extract

GARNISH
2 cups heavy whipping cream
1/2 cup coconut, toasted until golden

Preheat the oven to 350° F. Coat the bottom of a 9-inch by 13-inch baking dish with nonstick cooking spray. Line the pan with parchment paper.

To prepare the cake, combine the eggs, sugar, and salt in the bowl of an electric mixer and beat until tripled in volume. Quickly fold in the flour until just incorporated. Scrape the batter into the prepared baking dish.

Bake for 25 to 30 minutes, or until a toothpick inserted into the center just comes out clean. Let cool on a wire rack. Remove from the pan and discard the paper. Return the cake to the baking dish and poke many holes into the cake with a wooden skewer or large fork.

To prepare the sopping milk, mix together the coconut milk, condensed milk, rum, and almond extract. Pour the milk mixture over the cake, cover, and let sit in the refrigerator for at least 2 hours.

To serve, whip the cream until stiff peaks form. Serve slices of the cake topped with the whipped cream and toasted coconut.

Sour Cream Pecan Cake with Sweet Tea Ice Cream

SERVES 12

COFFEE CAKE
3 3/4 cups cake flour
2 1/2 teaspoons baking powder
1 1/4 teaspoons baking soda
3/4 teaspoon salt
15 tablespoons unsalted butter, at room temperature
1 3/4 cups plus 1 1/2 tablespoons granulated sugar
2 tablespoons vanilla extract
4 large eggs
2 1/2 cups sour cream

NUT LAYERS
3/4 cup granulated sugar
2/3 cup firmly packed brown sugar
1 1/2 cups pecans, toasted
2 tablespoons ground cinnamon

SWEET TEA ICE CREAM
1 quart sweet tea (1 quart brewed black tea, sweetened with 2 cups sugar)
4 cups heavy cream
1/2 cup granulated white sugar
8 large egg yolks

Preheat the oven to 350° F. Lightly butter a 9-inch by 13-inch baking pan.

Sift together the flour, baking powder, baking soda, and salt.

Combine the butter, sugar, and vanilla in a mixing bowl and beat until light and fluffy, about 5 minutes. Add the eggs, one at a time, beating well after each addition. Add the dry ingredients in thirds, alternating with the sour cream.

To prepare the nut layers, combine the white sugar, brown sugar, pecans, and cinnamon in a food processor and process until the nuts are finely chopped.

Spoon one-third of the batter into the prepared pan. Top with one-third of the nut mixture. Spoon in another third of the batter and top with another third of the nut mixture. Finish with the remaining batter and top with the remaining nut mixture.

Bake for 35 to 45 minutes, until a tester inserted near the center comes out clean.

To prepare the ice cream, bring the sweet tea to a boil. Boil until it is reduced in volume to 1 cup. Refrigerate until cool.

Combine the cream and sugar in a saucepan and heat until all the sugar is dissolved.

In a mixing bowl, beat the egg yolks until smooth. Slowly add the warm cream to the yolks, stirring constantly. Once the cream is added, cool the mixture. Add the sweet tea reduction.

Freeze the mixture in an ice-cream machine according to the manufacturer's directions.

To serve, slice the cake and microwave on high for 20 seconds. Add a scoop of ice cream to the top of each slice.

"Top Chef" fans watched with fascination as Richard Blais, faux-hawk always sharp and manners always mild, worked his "molecular gastronomy" magic on the food at hand, rising through the ranks to the final three. Blais had already impressed Atlanta foodies with wildly imaginative food at his own restaurants and others (Blais, Element, consulting gigs at One Midtown Kitchen and Piebar), having learned his liquid nitrogen trick (as well as the techniques to create his signature foie gras milkshake) in the kitchen of the master, Ferran Adria, at el Bulli in Spain. Kind to his competitors but brutally honest about himself, he announced to the "Top Chef" judges that he "clutched" at the final contest, essentially taking himself out of the competition. But Atlantans were thrilled to see him back at the helm in a new spot, with Blais' attention-getting takes on our own Southern cuisine. Blais has since left Home, but his menu remains. Along with only subtly-tweaked specialties like fried chicken, and macaroni and cheese with cauliflower, you'll find some multidimensional and surprising twists, such as a shrimp and grits layered and faceted with complementary flavors and textures. The little cottage houses a comfortable room of banquettes and several generations of well-heeled diners in a high-end Buckhead neighborhood.

WOODFIRE GRILL
Boca Negra Cake

SERVES 12

WHITE CHOCOLATE MOUSSE
1 cup heavy cream
1 tablespoon Grand Marnier
1 sheet gelatin or 3/4 teaspoon unflavored
  gelatin powder
1 tablespoon cold water (optional)
3 1/2 ounces white chocolate, chopped
1 cup heavy cream

CAKE
12 ounces dark (64 percent cacao) chocolate,
  finely chopped
1 1/2 cups sugar
1/4 cup Grand Marnier
1 cup unsalted butter, softened
5 large eggs, at room temperature
1 1/2 tablespoons all-purpose flour

BRACHETTI D'AQUI SYRUP
1 cup Brachetti d'Aqui wine, or you may
  substitute port or any red dessert wine
1 cup sugar

Founding owner and chef Michael Tuohy worked long and hard to enlighten Atlantans about the rewards of California-style cooking. By the time he left for California, just this year, after more than two decades of consistently innovative cooking, using fresh, organic, and (whenever possible) local produce and meats, the idea had really begun to catch on. Fortunately, Tuohy's restaurant will continue, along with his devotion to artisan cheeses, uncommon wines, and carefully farmed produce. An open fire is the heart of this restaurant with an open kitchen, where handmade pizzas, fresh fish, and assorted fowl and meats are cooked. The rest of the ochre-toned dining room has the warm, autumnal aura of a late-night campfire setting.

To prepare the mousse, combine the cream and Grand Marnier in a saucepan and bring to a boil. Meanwhile, if using the sheet of gelatin, soften in ice water for 5 minutes, then squeeze out excess water. If using powdered gelatin, sprinkle over the cold water and let soften for 5 minutes. Whisk the gelatin into the hot cream mixture.

Put the white chocolate in a heatproof bowl. Pour the hot cream mixture over the chocolate and whisk until smooth. Set aside until it reaches room temperature.

Whip the cream until it forms stiff peaks. Gently fold it into the chocolate mixture. Chill, preferably overnight.

Preheat the oven to 350° F. Lightly butter a 9-inch round cake pan and line the bottom of the pan with parchment paper; butter the parchment paper as well. Place the pan in a larger roasting pan; you will be baking the cake in a hot water bath.

To prepare the cake, put the chocolate in a heatproof bowl. Combine 1 cup of the sugar and the Grand Marnier in a saucepan and bring to a boil over medium heat, stirring occasionally. Pour over the chocolate and stir with a spatula until the chocolate is melted and the mixture is smooth. Stir in the butter, small pieces at a time.

Combine the eggs and remaining 1/2 cup sugar in a mixing bowl. Whisk until the eggs have doubled in volume. Slowly add the chocolate mixture, and whisk until well blended. Gently whisk in the flour. Pour the batter into the prepared pan, smoothing the surface. Pour enough hot water into the roasting pan to come up about 1 inch on the sides of the cake pan.

Bake the cake for exactly 30 minutes. Once the pan is cool enough to handle, remove the cake from the pan.

To make the Brachetti D'Aqui syrup, combine the wine and the sugar and simmer at low heat until the sugar dissolves, 15 to 20 minutes. Increase heat to medium low and cook 20 minutes longer

until the liquid is reduced by half.

Serve the cake warm or at room temperature, accompanied by the white chocolate mousse and Brachetti D'Aqui syrup.

Home Brew: The World of Coca-Cola celebrates chemist John Pemberton's sweet elixir, which he invented as a nonalcoholic alternative to his "French Wine Coca" after Atlanta introduced prohibition in 1886.

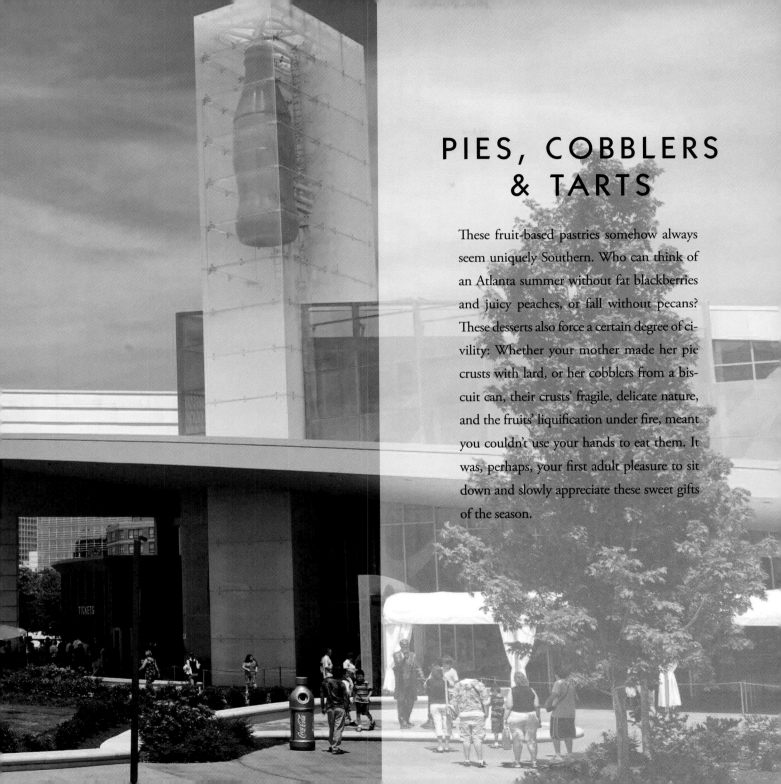

PIES, COBBLERS & TARTS

These fruit-based pastries somehow always seem uniquely Southern. Who can think of an Atlanta summer without fat blackberries and juicy peaches, or fall without pecans? These desserts also force a certain degree of civility: Whether your mother made her pie crusts with lard, or her cobblers from a biscuit can, their crusts' fragile, delicate nature, and the fruits' liquification under fire, meant you couldn't use your hands to eat them. It was, perhaps, your first adult pleasure to sit down and slowly appreciate these sweet gifts of the season.

WOODFIRE GRILL
APPLE CRISP

SERVES 12

FILLING
3 pounds Granny Smith apples, peeled and
sliced
2 cups raisins
1 1/3 cups granulated sugar
2 tablespoons all-purpose flour
4 teaspoons ground cinnamon
2 tablespoons unsalted butter, melted

CRISP TOPPING
2 cups all-purpose flour
1 cup granulated sugar
1/2 cup firmly packed light brown sugar
1 tablespoon ground cinnamon
1 teaspoon salt
1 1/2 cups unsalted butter, chilled and diced

To prepare the filling, combine the apples, raisins, granulated sugar, flour, cinnamon, and melted butter in a large bowl; toss to combine and set aside.

To make the topping, combine the flour, granulated sugar, brown sugar, cinnamon, and salt in a food processor and process briefly to mix. With the motor running, slowly add the butter in small amounts, mixing until the mixture has the texture and appearance of wet sand.

Preheat the oven to 375° F.

To assemble the dessert, transfer the apple mixture to a 9-inch by 13-inch pan. It will appear to be a lot of apples, but they do bake down, so be sure to pack them into the plate. Place the pie plate onto a sheet pan lined with aluminum foil for easy clean-up when the crisp boils over. Top the apple mixture with the crisp topping, firmly packing the topping, but leaving some gaps around the edges to allow heat to escape.

Bake for 30 to 45 minutes, until the topping is golden brown topping and the filling is bubbling.

Allow to cool for 15 minutes before serving.

"My therapist told me the way to achieve true inner peace is to finish what I start. So far today, I have finished two bags of M&M's and a chocolate cake. I feel better already."

—James Beard

> *"Vegetables are a must on a diet. I suggest carrot cake, zucchini bread and pumpkin pie."*
>
> —Ellen DeGeneres

CHERRY ALMOND TART

SERVES 8 TO 10

ALMOND PASTRY
1 cup butter, at room temperature
1 1/2 cups granulated sugar
1/2 teaspoon kosher or coarse salt
1/2 teaspoon ground cinnamon
5 ounces almonds, finely ground
1 large egg
1/2 teaspoon vanilla extract
2 1/4 cups all-purpose flour

CHERRY FILLING
4 cups dried cherries
1/2 cup port
1 cup water
1/2 cup heavy cream
1/2 teaspoon almond extract
1 large egg white, lightly beaten

To prepare the pastry, combine the butter, sugar, salt, and cinnamon in the bowl of an electric mixer fitted with a paddle attachment. Beat on low speed until smooth and well mixed; do not cream until light. Add the nuts and blend. Add the egg and vanilla and mix until just absorbed. Add the flour and mix until evenly blended. Form into two disks, one slightly larger than the other, wrap in plastic wrap, and chill for at least 30 minutes.

Preheat the oven to 325° F. Line a 10-inch fluted tart pan with parchment paper.

Put the large piece of dough between two pieces of parchment paper, and roll out to a circle of 11 to 12 inches—large enough to cover the bottom and sides of the tart pan—dusting with a little flour if the dough sticks to the paper. Gently remove the paper and fit into the prepared tart pan. Place a piece of parchment paper inside the pan and fill with pie weights or dried beans. Bake for 15 to 20 minutes, until the crust is light in color and still a little soft, not crispy. Remove the parchment and beans, return to the oven, and bake until the bottom is completely baked through, about 10 minutes. Cool completely.

Roll out the second piece of dough between the same two pieces of parchment paper. Place on a half sheet pan and freeze.

To prepare the filling, combine the cherries, port, and water in saucepan and bring to a simmer over low heat. Cook for about 10 minutes until all the liquid has been absorbed by the cherries. Transfer to a a half sheet pan and cool completely.

Whisk the cream and the almond extract together. Whisk until blended or until soft peaks form. Mix with the cherries. Spread evenly in the tart shell. Pull the half sheet pan of dough from the freezer, cut into 1/2-inch wide strips, and arrange on top of tart, creating a lattice pattern. Brush carefully with egg white.

Bake for 25 minutes, or until the lattice dough is baked through. Serve at room temperature or slightly warm.

RATHBUN'S
BANANA PEANUT BUTTER
CREAM PIE

SERVES 8

TART SHELL
1 1/2 cups all-purpose flour
1 teaspoon sugar
1/2 teaspoon salt
1/2 cup solid vegetable shortening
1/4 cup ice water

VANILLA CREAM
2 cups heavy cream
1/2 vanilla bean, split lengthwise and scraped
1 1/2 teaspoons cornstarch
1 tablespoon water
2/3 cup sugar
6 large egg yolks (reserve the whites for the
  meringue)

MERINGUE
6 large egg whites
1 1/2 cups sugar

ASSEMBLY
1/2 cup creamy peanut butter
2 bananas, sliced

GARNISHES
Caramel sauce
Mint leaves
Banana slices

To prepare the tart shell, sift together the flour, sugar, and salt. Crumble the shortening into the flour mixture with your hands until the shortening is in pea-size pieces. Make a well in middle of the mixture and add the water. Mix until the dough just comes together. Wrap in plastic wrap and refrigerate for 5 minutes.

Roll out the dough on a lightly floured surface to thickness of about 1/8 inch. Cut out into eight circles with a 4-inch circle cutter. Fit into eight 3/12-inch fluted tartlet pans with removable bottoms. Chill for at least 30 minutes.

Preheat the oven to 325° F.

Line the tarts with foil and fill with dried beans. Bake for 45 minutes, or until golden brown. Cool completely.

To prepare the filling, combine the cream and vanilla bean in a saucepan and bring to a boil. Remove from the heat and let steep for 30 minutes to extract the flavor from the bean. Meanwhile, prepare an ice bath by filling a bowl with ice and setting a smaller bowl inside. Stir together the cornstarch and water and set aside.

Add the sugar to the cream, stir well, and bring back to a boil. Whisk the egg yolks in a bowl. Slowly pour in the hot cream, whisking constantly. Return the mixture to the saucepan, pour in the cornstarch mixture, and cook until the custard thickens and just starts to bubble on the sides, about 2 minutes. Pour through the strainer into the ice bath. Let cool to room temperature, stirring a couple of times to bring the temperature down quickly. Refrigerate until you are ready to assemble the tart.

To prepare the meringue, combine the egg whites and the sugar in a heatproof bowl over barely simmering water and whisk until the sugar is dissolved and the egg whites reach 165° F on an instant-read thermometer. Beat with an electric mixer fitted with whip attachment on high speed until thick and cool. Place in pastry bag with star tip.

To assemble, spread about 1 tablespoon of peanut butter in each tart shell. Arrange the sliced bananas on top of the peanut butter. Fill the shells to the top with the vanilla pastry cream. Pipe the meringue on top of the tarts in any desired design. Brown the meringues with a kitchen blowtorch and serve drizzled with caramel sauce and garnished with mint leaves and banana slices.

WISTERIA
Pecan Pie with Ginger Whipped Cream

SERVES 8

PECAN PIE
1 1/4 cups pecan
9-inch pie shell, chilled
3 eggs, slightly beaten
1 cup light corn syrup
1/4 cup firmly packed brown sugar
1 tablespoon molasses
2 tablespoons unsalted butter, melted
2 tablespoons all-purpose flour
1/4 teaspoon salt
1 teaspoon vanilla extract
1 teaspoon vanilla seeds from 1 vanilla bean,
   split and scraped (Mexican vanilla beans are
   best)

GINGER WHIPPED CREAM
1 cup heavy cream
1 tablespoon confectioners' sugar
1 teaspoon ground ginger or 1 tablespoon
   chopped pickled ginger

Preheat the oven to 375°F.

Coarsely chop 1 cup of the pecans. Leave 1/4 cup whole. Spread the pecan inside the pie shell. Mix together the eggs, corn syrup, brown sugar, molasses, melted butter, flour, salt, and vanilla. Pour over the pecans. The pecans will rise to the top of the pie.

Bake for 45 to 50 minutes, until the filling has set. About 20 minutes into the baking, you may wish to tent the edges of the pie crust with aluminum foil to prevent the pie crust edges from burning. Remove from the oven and let cool completely.

Just before serving, prepare the whipped cream. Combine the cream, confectioners' sugar, and ginger in the bowl of an electric mixer fitted with a whisk. Beat until the cream has almost doubled and stiff peaks form. Serve slices of the pie with a dollop of the whipped cream.

Opened in 2001, this cool, brick-walled restaurant with the convivial bar has long been under-appreciated, as it serves almost grandmotherly versions of Southern favorites—if she were the sort to serve summer melon gazpacho or green tomato fries. Like that beloved set of Blue Willow dinnerware you inherited and still use often, Wisteria's old-school fare fits right in a contemporary environment, and seems all the newer for it. Chef-owner (and Johnson & Wales grad) Jason Hill's smart, modern Southern menu was always ahead of its time, but now that many of Atlanta's hottest restaurants are restoring formerly lowly Southern fare to its proper place of glory, Wisteria is getting a piece of the pecan pie.

MARY MAC'S TEA ROOM
Peanut Butter Pie

SERVES 8 TO 10

COOKIE CRUST
5 cups crushed chocolate creme-filled cookies
3 tablespoons unsalted butter, melted

PEANUT BUTTER FILLING
1 3/4 cups granulated white sugar
2 pounds cream cheese, at room temperature
1 cup peanut butter
3/4 teaspoon vanilla extract
1 1/3 cups heavy cream
1 large egg yolk

Preheat the oven to 300° F. Butter a 9-inch pie pan.

To prepare the crust, mix together the crushed cookies and melted butter until thoroughly blended. Press evenly along the bottom and up the sides of the prepared pan.

To prepare the filling, put the sugar in a mixing bowl. Add the cream cheese and peanut butter and beat with an electric mixer on low speed until fluffy and well blended. Add the egg yolk and mix well. With the beaters running, slowly add the heavy cream. Pour the batter into the pie shells.

Bake for 45 to 60 minutes, until a tester inserted in center comes out clean.

Chill before serving. Top slices with your favorite whipped topping.

When Mary ("Mary Mac") McKinsey opened her dining room in 1945, trolley cars still clanged down Ponce de Leon, and the Atlanta Crackers baseball team played at the field across from the old Sears building (now City Hall East). Since "restaurateur" wasn't considered a proper occupation for women, she called her place a "tea room," like many others around town often operated by war widows trying to raise children. Her hard work and handy midtown location helped Mary Mac's survive until the 1960s, when another ambitious businesswoman, Margaret Lupo, bought and expanded the restaurant. Attitudes toward working women hadn't improved much, but Lupo managed to secure financing and maintain quality and consistency to make Mary Mac's one of Atlanta's, and the South's, best-known and longest-enduring favorites. Since Lupo's hand-picked successor, John Ferrell, took over in 1994, there have been few changes. Patrons still fill out their own orders and first-timers still get free cornbread and pot likker (a kind of turnip-green ham broth) on request; the beans are still hand-snapped and the corn hand-shucked—but now you can also sip a glass of merlot or Sweetwater Pale Ale, an Atlanta microbrew, with your meal. Roadfood authors Jane and Michael Stern say the moist fried chicken "just might be the best in the South," and have included the restaurant on their honor roll since the 1970s.

PARK 75 AT THE FOUR SEASONS
PARK 75 SIGNATURE CHEESECAKE– SCENTED WITH ENGLISH STILTON, AND PORT REDUCTION BLUEBERRIES

SERVES 8

1 1/2 pounds cream cheese, at room
  temperature
4 ounces Stilton cheese
1 cup granulated sugar
7 tablespoons sour cream
1 1/4 teaspoons salt
3 1/2 tablespoons cornstarch
4 large eggs plus 2 large egg yolks

STEWED BLUEBERRIES
4 cups port
9 tablespoons granulated sugar
1 pint fresh blueberries

DRIED FRUIT AND NUT CRUST
1 cup unsalted butter
1 cup confectioners' sugar
1 large egg
1 1/4 cups cake flour
1 1/4 cups bread flour
1/3 cup sliced almonds
2 tablespoons finely chopped dried blueberries
2 tablespoons finely chopped dried apricots

Atlanta's most sumptuous Midtown hotel, the Four Seasons, with its sweeping marble staircase and intimate, clubby bar, offers some of the city's best celebrity-spotting. Park 75, the Four Seasons' restaurant, is a study of plush, formal dining, with thick, crisp linens and stunning floral arrangements. Voluble, chatty Chef Robert Gerstenecker is known for his precise, mosaic-like contemporary dishes, and pastry chef David Jeffries brings wit and whimsy to his careful craft. His "chocolate buffets" wow Valentine's Day guests. Park 75 also boasts one of the city's best "chef's tables": A dinner there puts you in the heart of the action, as an army of workers prepares the dining room fare, as well as a raft of room service orders.

Preheat the oven to 300° F. Spray an 8-inch square baking dish with nonstick cooking spray.

To prepare the cheesecake, combine the cream cheese, Stilton, and granulated sugar in the bowl of an electric mixer. Beat on medium speed for 3 minutes, scraping the bowl a couple of times to ensure a smooth mixture. Add the sour cream, salt, and cornstarch and mix on medium speed until smooth, scraping the bowl a couple of times. Add the eggs and egg yolks and mix on medium speed for 3 minutes, scraping the bowl a couple of times. Pour the mixture into the prepared baking dish. Place the pan in a shallow roasting pan and add water to come halfway up the sides of the baking dish.

Bake for 30 to 40 minutes, until firm. Let cool on a wire rack.

Freeze the cheesecake for 4 hours until firm. Portion while frozen to achieve nice clean edges when cutting, then thaw in the refrigerator.

To prepare the blueberries, combine the port and granulated sugar in a medium saucepan. Cook over medium heat until reduced by three-quarters. Remove from the heat and add the blueberries. Let cool, cover, and refrigerate.

To prepare the fruit and nut crust, cream together the butter and confectioners' sugar in an electric mixer until light and fluffy. Add the egg, scrape down the bowl, and mix until smooth. Add the cake flour, bread flour, almonds, dried blueberries, and dried apricots, and mix just to incorporate. Form into a flattened ball, cover with plastic wrap, and refrigerate until firm, at least 4 hours. Preheat oven to 350° F. Cover a cookie sheet with parchment paper.

On a lightly floured work surface, roll out the dough to a thickness of 1/16 inch. Cut into 4-inch

long triangles and transfer to the prepared cookie sheet.

Bake for 10 to 12 minutes. Cool on wire racks.

To assemble, slice the frozen cheesecake and let the slices thaw in the refrigerator. Place a wedge of nut crust on the plate and top it with a slice of cheesecake, slightly offset so that the crust is visible beneath the cheesecake. Spoon the blueberry port sauce onto the plate and serve.

FRENCH AMERICAN BRASSERIE
WARM APPLE GALETTE

SERVES 6

POACHED APPLES
4 cups water
2 1/4 cups lemon juice
1 teaspoon vanilla extract
1 cinnamon stick
2 star anise
2 cardamom pods
12 Fuji apples, peeled and cored

FRANGIPAN (ALMOND CREAM)
1 1/4 cups unsalted butter, at room temperature
1 1/4 cups confectioners' sugar
3 large eggs
1/4 teaspoon almond extract
1/4 cup dark rum
1 1/4 cups almond meal
6 tablespoons plus 1 teaspoon all-purpose flour, sifted

TUILE GARNISH
1 1/4 cups salted butter
1 1/4 cups granulated sugar
3/4 cup corn syrup
1 cup heavy cream
1 1/4 cups chopped almonds

GALETTE
1 (10-inch by 15-inch) sheet puff pastry, thawed if frozen
1/4 cup unsalted butter, melted
1 cup granulated sugar

Ice cream (caramel ice cream is recommended), to serve

The city's best French restaurant comes with a pedigree: In 1994, Brasserie Le Coze opened in Lenox Mall under the tutelage of siblings Gilbert and Maguy le Coze, owners of the famed New York restaurant Le Bernardin. Manager Fabrice Vergez helped make it a perennial favorite on critics' Top 10 lists. When a mall expansion took over Brasserie le Coze's space, Vergez bought the restaurant and relocated it to a new spot in a burgeoning corner of downtown. There, the concrete-and-glass exteriors sheath a traditional brasserie of white tiles, gleaming brass and polished mahogany, with beautiful Art Nouveau details. French American Brasserie has one of Atlanta's best rooftop terraces—a perfect spot to enjoy a French 75 cocktail while perusing the menu of steaks and French bistro classics like the specialty, skate wing in brown butter.

To prepare the poached apples, combine the water, lemon juice, vanilla, cinnamon stick, star anise, and cardamom pods in a large saucepan. Add the apples and simmer for about 20 minutes, or until tender. Lift the apples out of the liquid with a slotted spoon and cool on a sheet pan or large plate (be careful not to break apart the apples).

To prepare the frangipan, cream the butter with the confectioners' sugar until light and fluffy. Beat in the eggs, one at a time. Add the almond extract and the dark rum. Combine the almond meal with the sifted flour. Slowly add the flour mixture, beating to a smooth paste. Store in the refrigerator until you are ready to assemble the dessert. Frangipan can be made 1 day ahead of time and will keep for up to a week.

Preheat the oven to 350° F. Line a cookie sheet with parchment paper.

To prepare the tuiles, combine the butter, sugar, corn syrup, and cream in a small saucepan and bring to a boil. Add the almonds and bring back up to a simmer. Let cool. Form into 1- to 2-ounce balls (the size of a walnut) and place about 2 inches apart on the prepared baking sheet.

Bake for 10 minutes. Let cool at room temperature on the parchment paper until crisp. Store carefully because these will be fragile.

To prepare the galette, roll out the puff pastry sheet to a size about 1 1/2 times its original dimensions. Prick with a fork all over to reduce the rise and release air. Cut out six 5-inch rounds using a cookie cutter or a small plate. Place on two sheet pans.

Brush the melted butter onto the top of the puff pastry and bake for about 10 minutes, until

light brown. Spread an even layer of frangipan over the puff pastry and return to the oven for an additional 10 minutes, or until crispy.

Slice the apples 1/4-inch thick and assemble the cooled apples around the puff pastry sheet, leaving the edges exposed. Dust with the sugar and bake for another 10 minutes, or until warm.

Serve topped with ice cream and garnished with the tuiles.

This pretty little spot in shades of brown and pink is a showcase for the talents of former Bluepointe pastry chef Christian Balbierer. Part bakery, part café and all about chocolate, the space specializes in Balbierer's dark passion—but there are a few exceptions, such as this gorgeous little disk with "three lime" custard.

KEY LIME CUSTARD, GRAHAM CRACKER CRUST

SERVES 6

GRAHAM CRACKER PIE SHELL
3/4 cup finely ground graham cracker crumbs
3 tablespoons sugar
3 tablespoons unsalted butter, melted

KEY LIME FILLING
1 (14-ounce) can sweetened condensed milk
Finely grated zest and juice of 1 lime
3 extra-large egg yolks
1/2 cup Nellie & Joe's Famous Key West Lime Juice
4 Key limes, juiced

MERINGUE GARNISH (OPTIONAL)
1/2 cup egg whites (approximately 3 extra large eggs)
3/4 cup sugar

SUGAR GARNISH (OPTIONAL)
2 cups sugar
2 cups water
1/2 teaspoon cream of tartar
4 drops green food coloring

Preheat the oven to 325° F.

To prepare the pie shell, combine the crumbs, sugar, and butter in a bowl and mix until thoroughly combined; the mixture should feel like wet sand. Press into an 8-inch pie pan, covering the bottom and the sides in an even layer. Bake for 12 minutes. Cool completely.

To prepare the filling, combine the condensed milk and lime zest in the bowl of an electric mixer fitted with the paddle attachment. Mix on low speed for 1 minute. Add the egg yolks, one at time, mixing until fully incorporated after each. Stop the mixer and scrape down the sides. With the mixer on low speed, slowly pour in all three lime juices. Mix until fully combined. Pour into the pie shell.

Bake for 12 to 14 minutes, until the center has set. Allow to cool for 10 minutes, then refrigerate until fully chilled.

Lower the oven temperature to 200° F. Line a baking sheet with a Silpat or parchment paper.

To prepare the meringue, whisk the egg whites and sugar in a bowl to combine. Set the bowl in a saucepan of simmering water and heat until the sugar has dissolved and the mixture is smooth to the touch. Beat on high speed until stiff glossy peaks form. Using a pastry bag and a #6 piping tip, pipe 5 "kisses" onto the prepared baking sheet to make a flower meringue.

Bake for about 3 hours, or until the meringues are dry.

To prepare the sugar garnish, prepare an ice bath in the sink. Set out two Silpat mats or silicone liners. Combine the sugar and water in a tall saucepan and heat until the sugar is completely dissolved. Bring to a boil. Stir in the cream of tartar and continue to cook until the mixture reaches 265° F on a candy thermometer. Add the green food coloring and continue to cook until the mixture reaches 305° F. Immediately plunge the pot into a bath of ice water for 10 seconds.

Using a tablespoon, pour graduated dots of the sugar mixture onto a Silpat and allow to harden. Pour the remaining sugar mixture onto a Silpat and allow to cool for a moment. Then fold the

outside edges toward the center using a spatula. Continue folding the sugar, until it is cool enough to handle but still warm. Start pulling the sugar by holding it down with one hand and stretching it out with the other. Fold it over on itself and continue the pulling and folding until it begins taking on a glossy, shiny satin texture. You will need to pull and fold the sugar approximately 10 to 20 times to achieve the proper appearance. Pull into a ribbon and twist around the handle of a wooden spoon or similar item to achieve desired shape. Allow to harden and slide off. Sugar decorations can be made ahead of time and stored on parchment paper in an airtight container with a desiccant.

To serve, place the meringue garnish in the center of the pie, and add sugar dots around one side, as shown in the photograph. Place pulled sugar curls over the meringue garnish for additional decoration. Cut with a sharp knife, using a pie server to plate.

THE COLONNADE
COCONUT ICE BOX PIE

SERVES 7 TO 8

2 1/4 cups milk
1 cup sweetened coconut
1 tablespoon vanilla extract
1/2 cup granulated sugar
3 large eggs
2/3 cup cornstarch
1 baked 9-inch pie shell
2 cups heavy whipping cream
1/4 cup confectioners' sugar
1 cup toasted coconut

Incredibly, this Cheshire Bridge Road standby next to the Cheshire Motor Lodge has been serving Southern standards since 1927. The tried-and-true, time-capsule quality of Colonnade fare (fluffy yeast rolls, turkey and dressing, tomato aspic, potent highballs) draws a dedicated corps of regulars who seem to fear these things might disappear at any moment. With the sweet wait staff, many of whom have had long careers here, the Colonnade is an irreplaceable cornerstone of Atlanta culture.

Combine 2 cups of the milk, sweetened coconut, vanilla, and sugar in a saucepan. Bring to a simmer.

In a mixing bowl, combine the eggs, cornstarch, and remaining 1/4 cup milk. Beat until well combined. Very slowly add about one-third of the hot milk mixture to the cornstarch mixture, whisking constantly. Return the mixture to the saucepan. Cook over low heat, stirring constantly, until the mixture thickens; do not allow the mixture boil. Remove from heat and immediately pour into baked pie shell. Cool at room temperature for 15 minutes. Then refrigerate for 2 to 3 hours, until completely cool.

To serve, combine the heavy cream and confectioners' sugar in a bowl and beat until stiff peaks form. Evenly spread the whipped cream on top of the pie. Sprinkle with the toasted coconut.

For years, Atlanta's two Ritz-Carlton properties have served as engines revving up the city's dining scene. While the Buckhead Ritz's Dining Room is usually a pace car for the city's dining standards, the downtown Ritz's Atlanta Grill is a comfortable luxury sedan, with a more laid-back, informal environment—essential for the business crowd that frequents it. The Grill's new, young chef, Bennett Holberg, is that rarest of creatures: a native Atlantan. He's taken the clubby, masculine environment of the Atlanta Grill and added a bit of local color to the deep red leather banquettes. For the first time, the menu features some Southern specialties.

ATLANTA GRILL

Warm Peach Cobbler

SERVES 8

PEACH COMPOTE
1 1/2 cups pureed peaches
12 cups fresh sliced peaches
3 cups sugar
Pinch of ground cinnamon
1/2 cup cornstarch
1/2 cup water

MADELEINE MIX
4 cups all-purpose flour
3 1/4 teaspoons baking powder
3 cups granulated sugar
2 teaspoons finely grated lemon zest
2 vanilla beans, split lengthwise and scraped
10 large eggs

1 3/4 cups unsalted butter, melted
1/2 cup olive oil
1/4 cup peach schnapps (optional)

CRUMBLE
3 3/4 cups sugar
8 cups all-purpose flour
2 3/4 cups unsalted butter

CINNAMON-SUGAR
1 cup sugar
2 teaspoons ground cinnamon

Ice cream, to serve

To prepare the peach compote, combine the peach puree, peaches, sugar, and cinnamon in a saucepan and bring to a boil. In the meantime, make a slurry with the cornstarch and water. Add the slurry to the boiling compote and stir vigorously with a spoon to avoid lumps. Bring the compote back to a boil, then remove from the heat, transfer into a bowl, and set aside.

To prepare the madeleine mix, sift together the flour and baking powder.

Combine the sugar, lemon zest, seeds from the vanilla beans, and eggs in the bowl of an electric mixer fitted with a whisk attachment. Beat until the mixture is light and doubled in volume. With the mixer set on low speed, add the dry ingredients and mix until incorporated. Scrape the bowl with a rubber spatula and mix again until smooth.

Mix together the melted butter and olive oil, pour this into the batter while on medium speed, and mix until combined. Scrape the bowl with a rubber spatula and mix again until everything is incorporated. For additional peach flavor, add the peach schnapps, transfer the mixture to a container, refrigerate.

To prepare the crumble, combine the sugar, flour, and butter in the bowl of an electric mixer fitted with a paddle attachment. Mix on low speed until crumbly. Spread out in the bottom of an 8-inch by 10-inch baking pan. Place in the refrigerator.

To prepare the cinnamon-sugar, mix together the cinnamon and sugar. Set aside.

Preheat the oven to 350°F.

To assemble, fill 8 pint-size mason jars (3 1/2 inch diameter, 2 3/4 inch depth), one for each serving, or fill a 10-inch by 10-inch baking dish about two-thirds full with peach compote. Scoop or spoon the madeleine mix over peach compote until it covers the compote with a 1/4-inch layer. Loosen the crumble by rubbing it through your hands and cover the top of cobbler with the crumble.

Sprinkle the top with the cinnamon-sugar using 1 tablespoon per jar, or half the total amount if using the one large baking dish.

Bake for 15 to 17 minutes until the madeleine is springy to the touch and the crumble is brown. Serve warm with a scoop of ice cream.

Arch Comment: The Millennium Arch is a tribute to traditional architecture in Atlantic Station's modern live-work-play environment.

PUDDINGS & CUSTARDS

Soft and soothing as a mother's sigh, these comforting desserts are my first choice when I'm feeling low. Fortunately, that sentiment seems to be universal—there seems to be a creamy, unctuous treat from every corner of the globe. And despite its reputation as a Louisiana favorite, Atlanta seems to have appropriated bread pudding; you'll find it on a surprising number on the city's menus.

TAURUS
TOASTED PISTACHIO CRÈME BRÛLÉE

SERVES 6

1 cup pistachios
4 cups heavy whipping cream,
Pinch of salt
9 large egg yolks
3/4 cup sugar, plus 6 to 12 tablespoons for
    topping

Preheat oven to 325° F.

Spread out the pistachios in a single layer on a baking sheet. Roast for 12 to 14 minutes, until lightly toasted and fragrant.

Combine the pistachios, 4 cups cream, and salt in a medium saucepan. Bring to a boil, remove from the heat, and steep for 30 to 40 minutes.

Whisk together the egg yolks and 3/4 cup sugar in a large bowl until pale yellow.

Bring the cream back to a boil, remove from heat, and gradually pour into the egg yolk mixture in thirds, whisking constantly. Strain the mixture through a fine-mesh sieve and discard the nuts. Pour into six 6-ounce ramekins, filling each about three-quarters full. Place the ramekins in a roasting pan and fill with enough hot water to come halfway up the sides of the ramekins.

Bake for 35 to 40 minutes, until barely set around edges. Cool to room temperature. Transfer the ramekins to the refrigerator and chill for 2 hours.

Sprinkle 1 to 2 tablespoons sugar on top of each chilled custard. Using a kitchen blowtorch held 2 inches above the surface, caramelize the sugar. Serve immediately.

Dramatic and headstrong as the astrological sign, Taurus is where chef Gary Mennie draws a line in the sand. (Note to first-timers: You may circumvent the downstairs hostess stand and take the elevator directly to the restaurant.) There, the vibrant red leather banquettes and circular scheme, against a backdrop of glittering midtown skyline, virtually defy you to enter and be a part of the mix. The partially open kitchen makes the cooking a part of the dining room action. Beef, of course, is the raison d'etre, but in addition to his nightly "wood roasts" (short ribs, duck, pheasant), Mennie, who made his name at Atlanta's Canoe, also offers oysters, scallops, and salmon. Unlike many Atlanta chophouses, Taurus includes wonderfully complex sides with its main dishes, such as cauliflower gratin and wilted watercress with pomegranate ginger sauce. The "midtown meets Buckhead" address draws a mix of business folk with the landed gentry from nearby Ansley Park and lower Buckhead. In addition to the award-wining dinner menu, many critics also single out Taurus' fabulous desserts.

AGNES & MURIEL'S
BANANA PUDDING WITH TOASTED CINNAMON WALNUTS

SERVES 8 TO 12

PUDDING
1 1/4 cups all-purpose flour
1 1/2 cups granulated sugar
3/4 teaspoons salt
6 cups milk
6 egg yolks, lightly beaten
3 tablespoons butter, softened
1 1/2 teaspoons vanilla extract
4 cups vanilla wafer cookies
1 1/4 pounds ripe bananas, sliced 1/4 inch thick
2 cups heavy cream, whipped

CANDIED WALNUTS
1 pound walnut halves
2 cups sugar
1 tablespoon ground cinnamon
1 tablespoon freshly grated nutmeg

One peek at Agnes & Muriel's vintage early '60s dining room, outfitted with the wonderfully ersatz treasures that regularly filled garage sales until they became "mid-century modern" (Barbies, gold-flecked lamps, a hand-crafted "chandelier" of Mellamine cups and saucers) and you might fear you'd wandered into a scene from James Lileks' "Gallery of Regrettable Food." Fortunately, however, the specialties here aren't the freeze-dried wonder-foods of yore, but the Betty Crocker-style "food you wished your mother made," as their slogan says. (The restaurant is named for the original owners' mothers.) In addition to some fun cocktails (including a Bloody Mary with sake instead of vodka), tuck into new old-fashioned macaroni and cheese, fried green tomatoes, lemon-and-sesame seed collards, and a grilled Caesar salad.

Sift together the flour, sugar, and salt in a large mixing bowl. Add the milk gradually and stir well, making sure to remove any lumps. Transfer the mixture to a large saucepan and cook over low heat, stirring often, until just thickened, 10 to 20 minutes. When mixture begins to thicken, remove from the heat and set aside.

Whisk the egg yolks in a bowl and add 1 cup of the hot milk mixture while beating well. Return the egg mixture to the saucepan, add the butter and vanilla, and whisk until smooth. The egg yolks will be cooked without adding heat, if the milk mixture is sufficiently hot.

Layer the vanilla wafers, bananas, and custard mixture evenly in a 9-inch by 13-inch serving dish, making two layers. Refrigerate until completely chilled.

To make the candied walnuts, grease a sheet pan. Spray a cold nonstick skillet with nonstick cooking spray. Add the sugar, cinnamon, and nutmeg. Mix well. Begin to heat the sugar mixture over medium/low heat until the sugar is melted and a light amber color. Quickly add the walnuts and stir into hot sugar mixture, coating thoroughly. Spread the candied walnuts on the prepared sheet pan and allow to cool.

To serve, top each portion with whipped cream and a sprinkling of candied walnuts.

Georgia Muscadine Trio

SERVES 10

SORBET
2 pounds muscadine grapes
Juice of 2 lemons
1 1/2 cups sugar
6 1/2 tablespoons water
2 1/2 tablespoons glucose, or light corn syrup
 (purchase glucose online at lepicerie.com)

MUSCADINE COULIS
Skins of 40 muscadines
1/4 cup sugar
6 tablespoons water
1 vanilla bean, split lengthwise and scraped

PASTRY CREAM
4 1/2 cups milk
8 egg yolks
1 cup sugar
1 1/2 cups all-purpose flour

SOUFFLÉ
1 2/3 cups egg white (about 13 large eggs)
1/2 cup sugar
Flesh of 40 muscadines
2/3 cup of muscadine or grape schnapps
3 large egg yolks
2 tablespoons unsalted butter

To prepare the sorbet, combine the grapes, lemon juice, sugar, water, and glucose in a medium saucepan. Simmer until the grapes are tender, 20 minutes. Let cool slightly. Puree in a blender, then strain through a fine-mesh strainer. Chill until cold. Freeze in an ice-cream machine according to manufacturer's instructions.

Apply a liberal coating of softened butter to eight 6-ounce ramekins. Chill for 15 minutes. Apply a second coating of butter. Sprinkle sugar over the butter to cover generously.

To prepare the coulis, combine the muscadine skins, sugar, water, and vanilla bean in a small saucepan. Cook over medium heat for 20 minutes until tender. Remove the vanilla bean and puree in a blender until smooth. Strain through a fine-mesh strainer. Reserve in the refrigerator until you are ready to assemble the dessert.

To prepare the pastry cream, combine egg yolks and sugar in a saucepan and whisk until slightly white. Add the flour and whisk until smooth. Bring the milk to a boil and slowly pour the hot milk over the egg yolk mixture. Cook the mixture over low heat until it thickens, whisking continuously. Set aside to cool.

About 1 hour before serving, prepare the soufflé. Mix the egg whites and sugar. Set aside at room temperature. Combine the muscadine flesh with the schnapps and set aside to marinate.

Preheat the oven to 350° F.

When you are ready to bake, warm the pastry cream in a saucepan over low heat. Add egg yolks and butter mix until smooth. Strain the muscadines and stir in the liquid.

Beat the egg white and sugar mixture at full speed until stiff peaks form. Fold into the pastry cream mixture.

Place four marinated muscadines into each mold. Pour in the soufflé batter carefully (do not touch the sides of the molds).

Bake for 10 minutes. Serve the soufflés hot from the oven with the chilled coulis and the sorbet.

Elegant, intimate and luxurious. Sitting at a plush banquette in the recently updated, silk-walled Dining Room of the Ritz-Carlton Buckhead, you feel like the treasure nestled in the folds of a Fabergé egg. The only Atlanta fine dining establishment to have won the Mobil five-star award 11 times, the Dining Room is also one of only three restaurants in the nation to have won it for more than 10 years. Wine Spectator singled out the Dining Room's deep list for a 2008 "Best of" Award of Excellence. Chef Arnaud Bertholier smatters his French Mediterranean-inspired menu with touches from Africa and Asia, but his passion for local, seasonal ingredients has also steered him to some of the more exotic specialties of the American South. The experience here is formal and correct, but never stuffy—the dessert cart, with handmade lollipops and marshmallows, is as anxiously awaited as any kid's favorite ice cream truck.

BLUEPOINTE
TROPICAL THAI PARFAIT

SERVES 12

COCONUT PUDDING
2 1/2 cups coconut milk
1/2 cup sugar
1/4 cup heavy cream
3 1/2 tablespoons cornstarch
1 cup whipped cream

PIÑA COLADA SORBET
1 cup chopped pineapple
1 (13.5-ounce) can coconut milk
1 banana
2 cups simple syrup (see note below)
1 tablespoon rum

EXOTIC TUILE
14 tablespoons granulated sugar
1/4 cup all-purpose flour
2 tablespoons passion fruit puree
3 tablespoons mango puree
1/4 cup unsalted butter, melted

POACHED PINEAPPLE
2 cups pineapple juice
1 cup granulated sugar
1 vanilla bean, split lengthwise and scraped
1 tablespoon rum
1 pineapple, peeled, cored, and sliced into rings

Opened in December 1999, Bluepointe was the precocious blueprint for next-century dining, and quickly earned a "Best New Restaurant" nod from Esquire magazine. The sweeping, contemporary lines and tables overlooking a busy Buckhead section of Peachtree Street helped make Bluepointe the favorite business and neighborhood dining destination for the young, the stylish, the successful and those who want to be. The menu is as clarified and aquamarine as the stained glass over the always-happening bar: Asian-inspired cuisine with American touches, centering on fish and seafood. The sushi (and Bluepointe also has a separate sushi bar) is as strong a draw as the exotic varieties of cooked ocean fare and red meat, such as the house specialty of salt-crusted prime rib for two. The clockwork efficiency of the Buckhead Life Group's well-trained staff means you can often find a seat, even without a reservation.

To prepare the pudding, combine 2 cups of the coconut milk, sugar, and cream in a saucepan. Bring to a boil.

In a bowl, combine cornstarch and remaining 1/2 cup coconut milk, whisking to eliminate any lumps. Pour into the saucepan and cook until thick and no cornstarch flavor is present. Pour into 1 1/2-quart pan and refrigerate overnight.

Puree the pudding in a food processor. Transfer to a bowl and fold in the whipped cream. Put in a piping bag and set aside in the refrigerator.

To prepare the tuile, combine the sugar and flour in an electric mixer on low speed. Add the passion fruit and mango purees and blend well. Slowly drizzle in the melted butter and mix until just incorporated. Refrigerate for 2 hours.

Preheat the oven to 350° F. Line a baking sheet with parchment paper.

Spread the batter onto the prepared baking sheet. Bake until slightly golden, about 8 minutes. With a pizza cutter, cut 2-inch by 4-inch strips and wrap around a 1 1/2-inch circumference ring mold to create tubes, working quickly to mold the tuiles while they are still warm. If you don't have a ring mold, substitute a small glass jar, like the ones in which cocktail onions are packed.

To prepare the sorbet, combine the pineapple, coconut milk, banana, simple syrup, and rum in a blender and puree until smooth. Freeze in an ice-cream maker according to the manufacturer's directions.

To prepare the poached pineapple, combine the pineapple juice, sugar, vanilla bean, and rum in a nonreactive saucepan. Bring to a boil. Add the pineapple and simmer until tender, about 8 minutes. Remove the pineapple from the poaching liquid and let cool. Bring the poaching liquid to a boil and boil until reduced to a syrupy consistency. Strain.

To assemble, place 4 pineapple rounds on a plate, put the exotic tuile at the top and a slice of banana at the bottom of the tubes. Using the piping bag, alternate the coconut pudding with banana slices. Drizzle the syrup, place the coconut squares and the sorbet on the plate and serve.

CUERNO
ARROZ CON LECHE

SERVES 10 TO 12

ARROZ CON LECHE
8 cups whole milk
1 cup basmati rice
1 1/2 cups sugar
Pinch of saffron
Pinch of salt
1 vanilla bean
2 cinnamon sticks
Finely grated zest of 1 lemon
2 large egg yolks
1 cup heavy cream (optional)

BOUQUET GARNI
2 teaspoon toasted coriander seeds
1 teaspoon allspice berries
1 teaspoon black peppercorns
4 pods green cardamom
2 cinnamon sticks
1 vanilla bean
Zest of 1 lemon
Zest of 1 orange

MOORISH FRUIT
1 3/4 cups packed golden raisins
1 1/3 dried apricot halves, cut into large dice
1 cup chopped dried dates and/or figs
3/4 cup honey
3 cups dry white wine
1 tablespoon orange
   flower water

To make the arroz con leche, combine the milk, rice, sugar, saffron, salt, vanilla bean, cinnamon sticks, and lemon zest in a saucepan and bring to a boil. Reduce the heat and simmer until the rice is tender, about 15 minutes.

Whisk together the egg yolks in a bowl. Very slowly add a few cups of the hot milk mixture. Pour back into the saucepan, remove it from the heat, and stir well. The mixture should be hot enough to cook the eggs and thicken without heat. Transfer into a bowl and chill thoroughly. If the mixture is too thick after chilling, stir in the heavy cream until a desired consistency is reached. The desired texture will look like rice floating in melted ice cream. Remove the vanilla bean and cinnamon sticks before serving.

To prepare the bouquet garni, combine all the ingredients on a small square of cheesecloth. Gather together the corners and tie with a piece of kitchen string. Alternatively, place all the ingredients in a tea ball.

To prepare the fruit, combine the golden raisins, apricots, and dates in a nonreactive saucepan. Cover the fruit with white wine. Add the honey and bouquet garni. Bring to a boil, reduce heat, and simmer for 15 to 20 minutes, until the fruit is plumped and the liquid is syrupy. Cool, then add the orange flower water. Discard the bouquet garni.

Serve the rice and fruit chilled.

The latest addition to Riccardo Ullio's restaurant group (with Fritti, Sotto Sotto and Beleza) fills a much-needed culinary gap: Authentic Spanish paellas and tapas, with a long list of cavas and inventive cocktails. You can even drink from a porron, the little watering-can-style pitcher from which you pour directly into your mouth. This lively Midtown spot is drawing a young and restless crowd from its artsy neighborhood, who perch on tall stools with a view of the restaurant's centerpiece: a life-size metal bull sculpture, head low, as if he's just about to toss you across the room. The restaurant is drawing raves for its small plates and traditional entrees (including a rabbit and snail paella), as well as its custardy, home-style desserts.

5 SEASONS BREWING COMPANY
SWEET GRASS CHEESECAKE

SERVES 8 TO 10

POLENTA CRUST
1 cup unsalted butter, at room temperature
1/2 cup sugar
1 cups all-purpose flour
1 cups cornmeal
1/4 teaspoon salt

CHEVRE CHEESECAKE FILLING
1 pound fresh goat cheese (preferably from
   Sweet Grass Dairy), at room temperature
1 cup and 1 teaspoon sugar
4 large eggs
1 tablespoon vanilla extract
Finely grated zest of 2 lemons
Juice of 2 1/2 lemons

Much more than just a microbrewery, 5 Seasons was conceived by two chefs who had long wondered why good beer was so hard to find—especially with good food. The result is this singularly focused gastropub, so attentive to the earth's movements that the spent grain from beermaking is recycled in the housemade bread. 5 Seasons championed local ingredients since its opening in 2001, and prominently advertises "Georgia Organics" on its menu for everything from its grilled pizzas to its grass-fed, fresh-ground burgers. But you don't need to be a locavore to love this cheesecake, made with fresh goat cheese from Thomasville's prizewinning Sweet Grass Dairy.

Preheat the oven to 325° F. Wrap the outsides of eight 6-ounce ring molds with aluminum foil.

To make the polenta crust, beat together the butter and sugar until creamy. Add the flour, corn-meal, and salt and mix in until crumbly. Transfer to the prepared ring molds. Pat to form an even layer, about 3/8-inch thick, along the bottom and up the sides of the mold. Place the molds in a roasting pan and fill with enough water to reach halfway up the sides of the molds. Bake for 20 minutes, or until the crust is set and golden brown. Cool on a wire rack. Increase the oven temperature to 350° F.

To make the filling, beat together the goat cheese and sugar until creamy. Add the eggs, one at a time, beating just until incorporated before adding the next, scraping down the bowl and paddle three times to avoid lumps. Mix in the vanilla, lemon zest, and lemon juice. Pour into the prepared crust.

Bake for 5 to 15 minutes, until set.

Cool completely before serving.

MF BUCKHEAD
Mango Crème Brûlée

SERVES 6

1 large egg, plus 5 large egg yolks
1/2 cup sugar, plus more to sprinkle
1 1/2 cups heavy cream
Vanilla extract
1 cup mango puree
Fresh berries, to serve

Preheat the oven to 250° F.

Beat the eggs, egg yolks, and sugar in a bowl. Heat the cream and mix it very slowly into the egg mixture. Strain through a fine-mesh strain. Add vanilla to taste. Mix in the mango puree and pour it into 6 5-ounce ramekins. Place the ramekins in a shallow pan and boiling water into the pan to come halfway up the sides of the ramekins. Cover the pan with foil.

Bake for 35 minutes, until set. Chill for several hours, or overnight.

To serve, sprinkle sugar over the top of each ramekin and caramelize with a kitchen blow torch. Serve with fresh berries.

This audacious effort from young brothers Chris and Alex Kinjo (MF Sushibar, Nam) is one of Atlanta's most exciting new restaurants. Tucked behind a barely noticeable sign on the door of Buckhead's new Terminus Building, at the high-profile intersection of Peachtree and Piedmont, the curtain of metal beads at the foyer parts to reveal a gorgeous space of stacked walnut floors and silk panels, with the Kinjos' trademark attention to design. (Alex Kinjo personally created several components of the brothers' first two restaurants—you'll usually find him in a sharp suit and haircut, frowning at his Mac laptop at the bar.) Chris Kinjo, as ever, minds the sushi bar, where a phalanx of a dozen or more chefs prepares fish flown in from Tokyo's famed Tsukiji Fish Market. At Atlanta's only robata grill, chefs use bits of paper to hand-fan the fish as it cooks. Until recently, the Kinjos' restaurants seemed to feature desserts as an afterthought, but MF Sushibar's pastry chef is as experienced as the sake sommelier. Lisa Matsuoka, trained at the Culinary Institute of America, comes to MF Buckhead from New York's revered Le Bernardin.

ICE COLD

Coca-Cola

TRADEMARK
REG. U.S. PAT. OFF.

®

SOLD HERE

Cool Hangout: This big painted sign says you've arrived at Manuel's Tavern, where for more than half a century, politicos and policemen, salesmen and schoolteachers have gathered to watch baseball, drink and talk about the news of the day.

ICE CREAM, ICES & GELATO

If you can imagine August in Atlanta before air-conditioning, you can imagine the incomparable experience of eating homemade ice creams. Hand-cranked in the relative still of early evening, with fresh fruit and cane sugar or honey, they were the antidote to the hot, dusty day now behind you. Atlantans still love ice cream and frozen desserts, and in addition to their own cool memories, they can now explore the cold, sweet pleasures of other cultures.

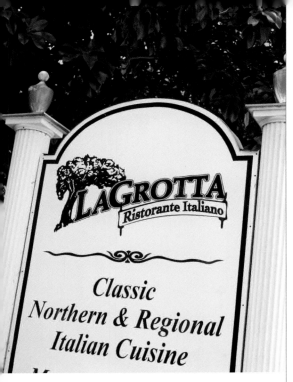

LA GROTTA
Zabaglione Gelato Tartufo

Marsala, a Sicilian fortified wine, is traditionally used to flavor zabaglione, a light dessert custard. In this recipe, rum is added for a more intense flavor.

MAKES ABOUT 3 1/2 CUPS

4 large egg yolks
1/2 cup granulated sugar
1 cup whole milk
1 cup heavy whipping cream
6 tablespoons dry Marsala
2 tablespoons dark rum
1 teaspoon vanilla extract
6 ounces chocolate
Confectioners' sugar

whipped cream, to garnish
mint, to garnish
fresh fruit, to garnish

Whisk together the egg yolks and sugar in medium bowl until thick, about 2 minutes.

Heat the milk and cream in medium saucepan over medium heat until the mixture bubbles at edges. Gradually whisk the hot milk mixture into yolk mixture, then return to the saucepan. Stir over medium heat until the custard coats the back of a spoon and reaches 170° F on an instant-read thermometer, about 6 minutes. Strain through a fine-mesh sieve set over another medium bowl. Stir in the Marsala, rum, and vanilla. Cover and refrigerate for at least 3 hours.

Freeze in an ice-cream maker according to the manufacturer's directions. Transfer to an airtight container. Cover and freeze until firm, at least 6 hours.

Once the gelato is firm, scoop out 3 1/2- to 4-ounce balls and lay on a flat cookie sheet covered with waxed paper. Refreeze.

Melt the chocolate in the top of a double boiler over barely simmering water. Dip each frozen gelato ball into the chocolate and transfer to the cookie sheet covered in waxed paper. Dust with confectioner's sugar and refreeze.

To serve, cut the gelato ball in half with a sharp knife. Garnish with whipped cream, fresh berries, and a sprig of mint.

Celebrating 30 years in business, this favorite old-school spot is as comfortable and well-heeled as its patrons. Tucked in the ground floor of a Buckhead high-rise, its dining room ringed with banquettes, La Grotta serves classic Italian dishes with panache. Despite the solid troupe of regulars, newcomers aren't made to feel like strangers. The uniformed wait staff, many with decades of experience here, is arguably among the best in town, never taking themselves—or you—too seriously. The cooking, however, is another matter. Chef Antonio Abizanda (co-owner and chef since La Grotta's opening) serves up sophisticated, complex and impeccably timed dishes, at a pace that never seems to either rush or delay diners. This is a very accommodating kitchen, with the goal of serving patrons and their wishes rather than imposing its own—special requests are welcome. However, you're always safe in the care of this food- and wine-loving wait staff, who arrive at your table armed and opinionated, ready to steer you through a charmed meal.

ANTICA POSTA
SEMIFREDDO AL TORRONE

"Semifreddo" is Italian for half-frozen, and refers to a number of chilled or part-frozen desserts, often with custard or ice cream.

SERVES 8 TO 10

5 1/2 ounces semisweet chocolate
5 1/2 ounces torrone (Italian nougat candy)
3 large eggs, separated
1/2 cup sugar
1/2 teaspoon unflavored gelatin powder
1 tablespoon water
1 1/3 cups heavy cream

Chocolate ganache, to garnish
Fresh strawberries, to garnish
Fresh mint leaves, to garnish

Combine the chocolate and torrone in a food processor. Chop until very fine.

Beat the egg whites until stiff peaks form, gradually adding the sugar as you beat.

Sprinkle the gelatin over the water in a small heatproof cup and let soften for about 5 minutes. Place the cup in a pan of simmering water until the gelatin is melted and the mixture is clear. Let cool to room temperature. Beat the heavy cream in another bowl until soft peaks form. Add the gelatin mixture and continue beating until stiff.

Beat the egg yolks for 10 minutes in another bowl.

Fold the egg whites into the whipped cream and until incorporated. Add the chopped mixture. Fold in the whipped egg yolks. Spoon into 4-ounce rectangular aluminum molds, cover with plastic wrap, and freeze.

Unmold the semifreddos and slice each into three 1-inch thick slices. Place one slice in the center of each plate. Shingle the other two slices toward the five o'clock position. Garnish with chocolate ganache, raspberries, and mint.

This pretty, perennial critics' favorite in a little yellow Buckhead cottage has a much higher profile than its modest exterior would seem to allow. The once-secret downstairs bar has been moved upstairs, into the light, but the energetic and intimate dining room remains as pleasurable as ever. Beyond the new bar, little has changed here in the years since Antica Posta's opening, when it became an immediate success with the press and the public. Then again, little has changed in most dining establishments in Florence, where maitre d' Marco Betti, chef Alessandro Betti, and family also operate a restaurant. Here you'll find, in season, the rare, delicately fried squash blossom as it is served in Tuscany—not stuffed with cheese nor rendered unrecognizable, but delicately crumbed, with the subtle, but unmistakable taste of zucchini. In addition to serving some of the most expert pasta dishes in town, Antica Posta offers traditional Florentine steaks—big, rare, and wood-grilled porterhouses, seasoned with extra-virgin olive oil.

RASPBERRY ICE WITH FRESH BERRIES AND PISCO SYRUP

Pisco is a brandy, thought to have been invented by Spaniards in the New World. It is still a popular drink produced in Chile, Bolivia, and Peru.

SERVES 4

RASPBERRY ICE	MACERATED BERRIES
2 pints raspberries	1 cup raspberries
Pinch of salt	1 cup blackberries
2 tablespoons fresh lemon juice	1 cup blueberries
1/4 teaspoon finely grated lemon zest	Pinch of salt
1/4 cup light agave syrup	1/2 cup light agave syrup
1 tablespoon pisco (Peruvian brandy)	1/2 cup pisco
1 cup water	
	Sprigs of mint, to garnish

RASPBERRY MERINGUES
4 teaspoons egg white powder

This fun and funky little tapas bar at the edge of Poncey-Highland is named for the Costa Rican expression that means (among other things), "life is great." Chef Hector Santiago samples from Spanish and Latin American cuisine to serve up these small plates, and the rocking Latin soundtrack is nearly as celebratory as the food. The ever-changing menu often includes traditional ingredients such as salted cod, the "Mexican truffle," huitlacoche, and several types of ceviche and pitchers of red and white sangria. Casual, comfortable and young at heart, Pura Vida is a reminder that the best mealtimes are carefree.

To make the raspberry ice, combine the raspberries and salt in a bowl and toss gently. Let the berries sit until they sweat. Add the lemon juice and zest and toss well. Add the agave syrup and pisco and let rest for 5 minutes.

Crush the berries with a fork, leaving it semi chunky, let sit for 1 hour.

Strain the crushed berries through a fine-mesh sieve pushing ever so lightly; you want to extract all the juice without any pulp and seeds. Reserve 1/4 cup of the juice for the meringue. Add water to the remaining juice. Strain the juice into a shallow plastic container and place in the freezer. After 30 minutes or so, pull out and break up the crystals with a fork. Continue freezing and stirring with a fork every 30 minutes until all the liquid has frozen into a slushy ice. Let freeze for another 30 minutes to firm up.

To prepare the meringues, warm the reserved 1/4 cup raspberry juice in a microwave for about 20 seconds; it should be warm, not hot. Add the juice to the egg whites and mix well. Whisk the egg whites until it forms stiff peaks. Spread the meringue onto parchment paper in an elongated teardrop fashion and dehydrate in the oven with the pilot on for 6 to 7 hours. If using an electric oven, set the temperature at 150°F, turning the meringue every 30 minutes for 3 to 5 hours. The meringue should be dry, light, shiny, and crisp. Store in an airtight container.

To make the macerated berries, combine the berries in a bowl, toss gently with the salt, and let sweat. Add the agave syrup and pisco. Refrigerate for 1 hour before serving.

To serve, fashion a bed of berries with a little juice on a cold plate or into cold glasses. Scoop the ice onto the berries; this is a very delicate ice with great texture, but it melts fairly quickly. Add the meringue strips and garnish each with a sprig of mint.

Burnt Honey and Gorgonzola Ice MIlk

SERVES 12

3/4 cup honey
1/2 cup water
2 cups heavy cream
2 cups low-fat (2 percent) milk
7 large egg yolks
1/4 cup sugar
1 ounce Gorgonzola

Heat the honey over medium heat in a deep, heavy-bottomed sauce pan. Honey will begin to bubble up as it heats. Swirl the pan every minute or so to keep it from overflowing and to keep it caramelizing evenly. Continue cooking the honey until the bubbles become extremely small, the color darkens to a deep mahogany, and the honey begins to smell burned and smokes slightly. Remove the pan from the heat. Very slowly and carefully, pour in the water a few drops at a time. The honey will bubble briskly. Let sit for 10 minutes.

Add the cream and milk to the honey and place over low heat. Warm until hot but not boiling.

Whisk the egg yolks and sugar together until thickened and pale yellow. Very slowly add about half of the cream mixture to the yolks while whisking constantly. Return to the cream mixture and cook over low heat, stirring constantly, until the custard thickens slightly and coats the back of a wooden spoon. Strain through a fine-mesh strainer and chill until cold, preferably overnight.

Freeze the Gorgonzola. Cut into small pieces with a heavy chef's knife. Return to freezer.

Freeze the ice-cream mixture in an ice-cream machine according to the manufacturer's instructions. Fold the frozen Gorgonzola pieces into the ice cream and freeze overnight to harden.

Housed in what was once the home base for the Atlanta Fencing Club, Ecco is a reminder that midtown always had a sophisticated edge, even before the recent explosion of luxury apartments, condos and lofts. Just off Peachtree Street, Ecco serves as a handy meet-up before a show at the Fox or a concert at Symphony Hall, and the late-night menu refuels many a de-energized party-goer. The bar seems as hot a destination as the dining room, with several hipsters often crowded around a small table for hours at a time. The European-inspired menu isn't overly complicated, relying on the best ingredients and accomplished techniques for familiar flavors in new combinations.

5 SEASONS BREWING COMPANY
COUNTRY FRIED PECAN–CRUSTED PEACH ICE CREAM WITH DRUNKEN PEACHES AND BLUEBERRY CARAMEL

SERVES 8

DRUNKEN PEACHES
1/4 cup honey
1/4 cup sugar
1/2 vanilla bean, split lengthwise and scraped
4 Georgia peaches, peeled and diced
Juice of 1 lemon
1/2 cup bourbon

PEACH ICE CREAM
2 cups heavy cream
2 cups whole milk
1/2 vanilla bean, split lengthwise and scraped
1 cup sugar
8 large egg yolks

BLUEBERRY CARAMEL
1 cup sugar
Juice of 1 lemon
Pinch of sea salt
1/2 cup pureed blueberries
1/2 cup heavy cream
2 teaspoons unsalted butter

CRUST
3/4 cup pecans, crushed into small pieces
3/4 cup dried bread crumbs
2 large eggs
2 tablespoons milk

Canola oil, to deep-fry

To prepare the peaches, combine the honey and vanilla bean in a nonreactive over low heat and cook for 5 minutes. Remove from the heat and add the peaches, lemon juice, and bourbon. Return to low heat and cook for 10 minutes. Remove the vanilla bean, divide between two bowls, and cool, reserving half for the ice cream and half for plating.

To prepare the ice cream, combine the cream, milk, and vanilla bean in a saucepan and heat over medium heat to 175°F.

Beat the egg yolks and sugar until pale in color. Slowly add about one-third of the simmered cream mixture to the yolks and whisk until incorporated. Slowly whisk the yolk mixture back into the cream mixture and cook over low heat until the custard will coat the back of a spoon and registers about 160°F on an instant-read thermometer, about 1 minute.

Pass through a strainer to remove any lumps and the vanilla bean. Cool in an ice-water bath. Freeze in an ice-cream maker according the manufacturer's directions. Transfer to a freezer container and freeze for 1 hour to set. Fold in half of the drunken peaches and return to the freezer to set.

To prepare the caramel, combine the 1/3 cup of the sugar and lemon juice in a saucepan over medium-high heat. Stir until the sugar dissolves. Slowly add the remaining 2/3 cup sugar and salt and continue cooking and stirring, until all the sugar has dissolved and the color is a reddish mahogany in color. Carefully and slowly add the blueberry puree and whisk to incorporate. Add the cream and butter. Bring to a boil. Remove from the heat and cool. When cool, pass the caramel

through a fine-mesh strainer.

To prepare the crust, mix together the pecans and bread crumbs in a bowl. In another bowl, beat together the eggs and milk until blended.

To make the fried ice cream, use a 4-ounce scoop to make 8 scoops of the peach ice cream. Place the scoops on a baking sheet lined with parchment paper and return to the freezer until the scoops are cold and have set, about 1 hour.

Roll the ice cream balls in the pecan crumb mixture and return to the freezer until thoroughly re-frozen.

Coat the ice cream balls with egg-milk mixture and roll one more time in the pecan mixture. Return to the freezer until set.

To fry the ice cream, heat 3 inches of canola oil in a deep saucepan to 375° F. Carefully slide the frozen crusted ice cream in the oil and cook for about 1 minute, or until golden brown. Fry two at a time. Remove with a slotted spoon, drain briefly on paper towels, then plate immediately.

Serve with remaining drunken peaches and blueberry caramel.

PEACH BELLINI GELATO

*"Ice cream is exquisite.
What a pity it isn't illegal."*

—Voltaire

SERVES 15

3 cups whole milk
Pinch of salt
7/8 cup (14 tablespoons) sugar
6 large egg yolks
1/3 cup peach puree or nectar
3/4 cup peach schnapps
1/3 cup champagne, preferably demi sec

Mint to garnish
Fruit to garnish

Bring the milk and salt to a boil in a medium saucepan over medium heat.

Whisk together the sugar and egg yolks in a bowl. Slowly add the milk mixture, constantly stirring with a whisk. Add the peach puree and mix well. Place this bowl in an ice bath using another larger bowl filled with ice and water and stir occasionally until the mix is cool. Stir in the peach schnapps and champagne. Freeze in an ice-cream machine according to manufacturer's directions, until the mixture has the texture of soft-serve ice cream. Freeze until firm.

INDEX

My thanks to Janice Shay and Deborah Whitlaw Llewellyn, whose experience and sharp eyes helped shape this book. I also appreciate the support and encouragement of my friends and colleagues, including, especially, Susan Percy, editor of *Georgia Trend* magazine.   —*K.R.*